HUMAN
RESOURCE
MANAGEMENT

-HUMAN RESOURCE MANAGEMENT-

AN ROI APPROACH

RAY A. KILLIAN

A DIVISION OF AMERICAN MANAGEMENT ASSOCIATIONS

658.3
K48h

To my wife,
who understands empathy
and practices effective human relations

Library of Congress Cataloging in Publication Data

Killian, Ray A
  Human resource management.

  Includes bibliographical references
  1. Personnel management.   I.   Title.
HF5549.K478   658.3   76-7058
ISBN 0-8144-5415-1

Contents

Preface

The time has come when the ultimate test of managerial effectiveness is its return on investment in its human resources. The time is *now* when employees insist on meaningful participation in company affairs. Employees at all levels control options that determine company success or failure, and they will exercise these options in accordance with what the company does for them.

This book reflects my conviction that companies and people want results. It is short on unproved theory but long in the practical areas "where the rubber meets the road." It will work! It meets the needs and self-interests of employees and companies. It can help management improve employee relations, productivity, leadership effectiveness, human compensation, and—of equal importance —it can lead to job enrichment. It advocates concepts, plans, and actions that enable everyone concerned to attain a maximum return on his or her personal investment of time and effort. It shows management how to build bridges to achieve today's results and go on to meet tomorrow's human challenges.

People management today involves totally new leadership dimensions, demands, and risks. Human-oriented decisions must now be made with an eye to the potential consequences involving legal compliance and investigations, employee relations, customer response, productivity, human costs, outside group pressure, and economic impact. Too often, a solution in one of these areas can create numerous new problems in others.

The morality issues inherent in hiring, compensation, working conditions, leadership, promotions, and discharges require the highest form of value judgment on the part of management.

People-related action demands careful overall planning and cautious but firm leadership.

This book addresses itself to a comprehensive, total approach to people problems through achieving a return on investment in human resources, human time being the largest single operating cost for most enterprises. The book confronts the most complex and challenging demand made on management—that of managing people. In today's humanized era, every manager from the chief executive of the largest corporation down through the first-line supervisor in the smallest unit needs to understand and respond to the impact that return on investment in human resources has on both daily operating activity and economic results.

Maximizing return on investment in people does not mean exploiting, manipulating, or taking advantage of employees. Rather, it means providing the highest form of benefit a company can offer its employees—a systematic, organized approach to guaranteed opportunities for the full use of talent and potential. Such an approach offers the individual an opportunity to achieve an appropriate return on his or her own investment of time and effort through greater economic and personal rewards. The company in turn benefits as its production, sales, and profit goals are achieved.

This book also provides the framework for realistic human resource planning and management. It contains numerous guides, lists, charts, illustrations, examples, and specific steps and recommendations based on years of firing-line experience. It attempts to put all the pieces together in a logical, practical, sequential process to help the manager take appropriate action regarding all areas related to people. Its use as a planning guide should result in more effective, profitable human activity and should provide a realistic operating system for individual managers. The overall goals of the organization, its leaders, and its individual employees can best be advanced and achieved through the implementation of the human resource concepts advocated.

The concepts and guides in this book should be of special concern to top executives who are responsible for the return on investment in human resources and overall employee relations, to middle managers who must achieve quantitative results and teamwork within their units, and to individual employees who will insist on a personal ROI as it might affect their careers, pay, growth, job satisfaction, and that portion of their time sold to the company. Educators should be interested because the book reveals the type of education that will best qualify individuals to become effective contributors in tomorrow's world. All enterprises and institutions, profit making as well as nonprofit—such as government, religious, and medical—should also be acutely concerned with the efficiency of human resource utilization and the contribution a higher level of human resource management can make to goals of the organization.

Although nontechnical, the book does provide specific action programs. It seeks to enable every employee and manager to understand his or her role in the more effective use of human resources and the benefits that will accrue to everyone involved. Hopefully, it will provide the pathway through which management and employees will discover the compatibility of their mutual objectives and bring about the type of energized, cooperative teamwork that will lead to greater mutual goal achievement. It will not achieve the millennium, but it should cause attention and resources to be directed realistically toward meeting the dynamic human challenges of the final quarter of the twentieth century.

RAY A. KILLIAN

1
The critical
importance of people

People. Human resources. Rising cost of human time. Job disenchantment. Making jobs fit for people. Search for more meaningful work experience. Employee hostility. Puzzling people problems!

These words and thoughts plague and frustrate most employees and leaders associated with organized human activity. Yet there is probably no other area of modern society that has had less truly professional, scientific, and organized attention than the critical factor of human resources. The picture has been one of piecemeal solutions. Bromides and panaceas have been advocated by amateurs and experts. Seldom has a total professional approach been taken to the management of human resources.

But the humanized era has arrived. The industrial society is rapidly becoming the human society. The age of consumerism and employeeism is here. The remainder of the twentieth century will be known as the people generation. The focus of planners, managers, and social scientists will shift from machines, buildings, economics, and markets to people.

In the future the effectiveness of business and its executives will be measured in human terms—the extent to which the enterprise contributes to society and the individuals associated with it. Achievement will not be judged by numbers and dollar marks alone but also by its impact on the quality of human life. Business activity and management's success criteria will have a new frame of reference, new bench marks for measuring results. Expectations will rise from the drudgery of subsistence to visions of the good life.

Human beings in a free, affluent society, enlightened concerning the potential of "their one time around," will insist on totally new forms of organization, leadership, participation, and personal benefits. The company or the individual leader who fails to accurately gauge and respond to these changed dynamics will be shunned and forgotten.

COMPANY ACTION IN THE HUMAN ERA

The enterprise, by its policies and actions, and the manager, through his or her decisions and leadership, must link plans and activity to the human resource concept. To be effective, this action must be creditable and must be based on the following conditions, which will become facts in the human era.

—Decisions regarding people—employment, pay, promotions, and job satisfaction—will assume the level of moral and ethical issues.

—Human resource activities will not be limited to economic considerations, but will reflect the deeper creed, philosophy, and mission of the enterprise.

—The company will recognize that its greatest potential for growth, profit, continuity, and good will is locked within the talents and efforts of its people.

—Employees will insist on meaningful participation in decisions and changes that might influence their jobs and lives.

—Company caste systems will be homogenized to the extent that there will be little distinction between management and employees based on job titles, working conditions, job privileges, benefits, and job security.

—The company will have fewer "inalienable rights or prerogatives."

—The company must merit the presence, the support, and the response of employees and customers.

—Employees will insist on many considerations and rewards beyond fair pay and employee benefits.

—Employees will feel that they are entitled to develop and use to the fullest extent their talents and minds and that they should work only for the company that makes this possible.

—The criteria for company success and managerial effectiveness will depend principally on the management of human resources.

Company organization, policy, practice, and leadership must reflect this new era. Results now, and throughout the rest of this century, will depend on providing an environment for the full development of people. Policy and action must reflect the influence of people over an organization's effectiveness.

WE'RE IN THE PEOPLE BUSINESS!

The typical manager's cliché is, "We're in the people business here. People are our most important asset." But, on the basis of company practices, what do employees believe about the company? They see dusty creeds and lip service that do not mesh with reality. Actual decisions and action too often demonstrate that the sole concern of the company is not for people but for economics.

If a company believes that it is in the people business, its total operation will reflect this belief. The orientation will be responsive to people considerations. Training and development will provide for people growth and use of potential. Leadership will give recognition and reward on the basis of merit. Individuals will have the opportunity to voice their opinions on action that will influence the future of their jobs. The whole human resource system will be designed and operated to balance people concerns with economic results.

PEOPLE DETERMINE RESULTS

Employees and the public have needs and concerns that must be met. People now have many legal rights and feel entitled to many other considerations beyond legal requirements. They expect the company to provide acceptable working conditions, a humanistic organization, and the opportunity for growth—and they will minimize their productive effort, or leave, if conditions continue to be unsatisfactory.

I want to stress here that people consideration means operating a profitable, growing company. It does not mean tolerating sloppy work or halfhearted effort. It means making the decisions that have to be made in the best short- and long-range interests of everyone associated with the company. A union leader observed, "Yes, I can force the company to pay $15 an hour. But it won't be of much benefit if there are no jobs." Only successful companies can provide what employees want: pay, benefits, opportunity, growth, security, and the chance to make a meaningful contribution.

In meeting human requirements, the company does not have to sacrifice its self-interest; rather, the type of work-a-day world the employee wants can also serve the best interests of the company. Companies such as IBM, known as national leaders in growth and profit, are also leaders in human resource planning and attention to people needs. One of IBM's operating tenets is to maximize return on investment in all resources—financial and human. Any resource not fully utilized constitutes waste and mismanagement. Full utilization of the intelligence, the talents, the time, and the potential of people provides the company with its most important opportunity for achieving its financial goals.

Those who control company activities should recognize that people concerns must be served. Company managers and decision makers have the unique opportunity of building and operating organizations that can provide for the affirmation of individuals and at the same time attain the quantitative objectives of the company.

THE COMPANY AS A DEMOCRACY

There are many elements in a free society that survive and thrive only if they merit continued support. The politician is elected to office, or is reelected, only if the voters believe that he deserves their vote. Getting the office is dependent on the good will and support of someone outside himself.

Through the same process, employees and customers determine which companies stay in business. Generally speaking, no employee *has* to work for a particular company. Few customers *have* to go into a particular store to transact business. The company functions as a democracy in that it must deserve the "vote" of its employees and customers. Without that vote, the company cannot continue to exist. Throughout the company, there should be an awareness of and response to the absolute necessity of the presence and support of employees and customers. Everything the company does should merit the confidence of its "voters."

ACHIEVING COMPETITIVE SUPERIORITY

In a competitive, free-market environment, dynamic forces operate to determine the relative success or failure of a company. In the final analysis, these control factors can all be condensed under the general term "competitive edge" or "superiority." The customer, having freedom of choice, will seek out the company with the best product or service. The financial institution will lend its limited financial resources to the company with the best reputation and track record. The supplier of raw materials and services will give first priority to those companies that have demonstrated integrity in paying bills and living up to contractual obligations.

In *The Achieving Enterprise,* William F. Christopher writes that it is no accident that certain companies listed by Dun & Bradstreet, Inc. have shown superior results. He indicates that the following characteristics are generally found in superior organizations:

1. A strong sense of identity felt throughout the organization.
2. Openness to change.
3. Authority diffused broadly throughout the organization.
4. Ideas evaluated more on their merit than on their origin.
5. A strong sense of support of the employees for their company, of the company for its employees, and of the employees for each other.
6. Flexible organization forms.
7. Orientation to achievement more than to procedures or ritual.
8. Open communications throughout the organization—up, down, and across.
9. Commonly held understanding of company values and objectives.
10. Emphasis on and programs for the development of people.
11. Meetings oriented primarily to problem solving, not to win–lose decisions.
12. Broad content in individual jobs.
13. High performance standards.[1]

It is the total superiority of products, services, reputation, and business relationships that affords a particular company the competitive

[1] AMACOM, 1974, p. 19.

edge. It is analogous to the parable of the talents—those companies that have put their talents to work and have achieved a competitive advantage will experience accelerated growth. Those companies that fail to maintain competitive excellence will experience slowed growth and gradual loss of position in the market.

The company's compelling and continuous thrust must be to produce and deliver the best product and service. It must search for and implement those forms of human organization, leadership techniques, and operating processes that will encourage customers to purchase from and employees to work for the company. A review of the rise and fall of companies reflects this influence at work. A list of national companies in the top 100, based on sales, profits, and rate of growth, reveals a rapid turnover in the span of just a few years. Companies seem to forget, or lose the ability to keep implementing, those elements on which their success was built.

THE ROLE OF HUMAN RESOURCES

To understand the critical importance of people in the operation and competitive position of the company is to recognize that the human element and the company are synonymous. The company and its progress are forms of human activity. Most often company failure is one of people failure. People fail to accurately gauge the forces of change and thus make the wrong decisions. People fail to find a need and meet it. It is people who employ, promote, organize, lead, and decide which products are produced and advertised and where the products will be marketed. The decisive difference in service is determined by people.

Too many companies say that people are their most important product and then disregard this fact in their priorities. They fail to provide the opportunity for people to make their full contribution. They discourage the ideas and creativity of people. They forget that people are decisive in the current results and future status of the company.

Managers are inclined to devote their energies, time, and attention to the "more practical" problems of production, not people; marketing, not employees; computers, not co-workers. While difficult in themselves, these "more practical" problems often do yield more satisfying and measurable results. Managers thus practice a system of priorities that places people importance low on its scale of values.

PEOPLE AS AN OPERATING COST

Rensis Likert's work and the human resource accounting program at The University of Michigan have focused on the dollar value of people. This has been done by asking, "Suppose that your company suddenly discovered that it still possessed all its plants, equipment, inventories, stores, and other physical assets—but no personnel except the president. If you had to rebuild the human organization from this point, how long would it take? How much would it cost in terms of direct expense, lost production, lost sales, and lost profits?"

How important are a company's human resources? Total dollar cost, as a percentage of operating expense alone, makes the purchase of human time the key to financial results. Typically the total company expense for human time and presence on the job amounts to 70 percent of the total cost of operation. This figure includes the direct cost of payroll and employee benefits but does not include the accompanying costs of employment, training, and the like.

What priority should be given to human resources? Consider the facts. If the total annual operating expense for a company is $40 million, 70 percent of this would amount to $28 million. For five years this cost would be $140 million. This figure makes no allowance for company growth or increase in wage rates and employee benefits. Actual experience indicates that normal growth of the company and people-related costs over a five-year period might push the figure closer to $200 million.

If the company anticipates purchasing $200 million worth of human time during the next five years, how much planning and commitment of management attention are needed? I believe that the human element deserves the number one priority of management. The company can go all out to control expenses in production, freight, paper flow, utilities, and so on but still achieve only limited results unless it concentrates on the largest, most flexible element of operating cost—human time.

The two key elements of return on investment (ROI) in people are the number of dollars spent and what the company gets in return for this purchase. The company should, therefore, focus attention on controlling costs and maximizing the productive contribution received in return for this expense.

UNIQUENESS OF THE HUMAN RESOURCE

The uniqueness of the human resource requires a totally different type of attention from management. The human resource has characteristics that provide the company its greatest challenge and opportunity:

—It cannot be purchased en masse, but individually—one person at a time.

—It cannot be hoarded or warehoused, but it must be made available on an hourly and daily basis.

—It is perishable in that it must be used currently; if it is not needed or if it is unproductive today, it is still consumed and is not available for future use.

—The company must, through its reputation and efforts, solicit the human resource.

—Each individual has the option not to apply for a job, not to report for work each day, and not to expend effort.

—The company must, through its organization and programs, merit the presence and contribution of the human resource.

—The individual has the freedom to resign, and the company has certain options for discharging the individual. Thus the relationship is fragile, with each party having the right to terminate it.

—The human resource represents both short- and long-range investment on the part of the company, an investment in which the profitability and life span are unpredictable.

—The availability of the human resource, its contribution, and its return on investment depend on appropriate attention and response by management.

A company's human resource is fragile, its relationship is delicate, its contribution is unpredictable, and its permanency uncertain. The burden is on those people who control and operate the company to recognize the uniqueness of this resource and to deserve its presence and full commitment.

A MATTER OF MORALITY

The newest, most significant human resource consideration is morality. This does not mean morality as implied by religious creeds but the treatment of people. The order of creation, as set forth in most major religions, emphasizes that people are the highest order of creation and therefore should be treated accordingly. Although religious and humanistic leaders have sought to promote this concept, it has seldom been given wide-range implementation.

Early commercial and industrial society made little impact on the general disregard for people. But today, through mass affluence, increased education, legal requirements, and freedom from the slavery of ignorance and poverty, the "people will be served" era has arrived. The mistreatment of a group or a single individual can cause heavy financial cost to a company. This can occur through legal investigations and fines, employee hostility, public criticism, and consumers' failure to purchase the company's product or service.

The company and its leaders must be concerned with operating efficiency and profit. But the moral considerations for people must be of equal or greater concern. Making too much profit at the expense of employees and customers subjects the company and often its entire industry to public wrath and, in many instances, permanent legal constraints. Failure to be competitive in terms of salaries and benefits subjects the company to loss of employees and production.

Companies and managers can no longer fail to meet their moral obligations to people and society without risking severe, disabling repercussions. The recognition of this reality has led companies to establish personnel departments, engage in human resource planning, provide high-quality training and development programs, and structure their organizations to ensure an acceptable form of human morality in their treatment of people. Appropriate response to human morality issues reflects not only the new awareness of the humanistic environment but also the self-interest of the company in terms of its growth, profit, and public good will.

THE NEED TO GUARANTEE ROI

The performance and survival of the company depends on a return on investment in human resources. Significant cost savings and productivity improvements are strong arguments for investments in human resource planning programs. The availability and performance of people depends on the work environment, opportunities for growth, and treatment provided by the company.

Thus the future of the enterprise and the self-interest of its individual employees hinge on ROI in human resources. The most reasonable guarantee that this will occur is to have an appropriate system in operation, which involves:

Control of expenditures for human resource time.

Full utilization of the time and potential of people.

A human organization that motivates people and promotes productivity.

Policies, practices, and leadership that reflect concerns for people.

A program for retaining profitable human assets.

A company that plans for and expects top results and thus provides job security, growth, and benefit for all employees.

A company that demonstrates a priority concern for people as it moves forward to the achievement of its goals.

Human resource planning should give equal consideration to all levels and categories of people in the company. Managers, executives, and supervisors are human assets, too. These employees also have needs and expectations. They can be mistreated. They are subject to loss of interest and separation from the company. Thus constant effort should be exerted for the construction and operation of a humanistic organization that will provide for the affirmation of company expectations as well as for those of all its people.

2
Emerging challenges

Change has been the watchword since World War II. Dramatic changes have taken place in technology, mechanization, electronics, and forms of human organization. Perhaps the greatest challenge associated with change has occurred in the relationships and expectations of people. The most severe test of company harmony and survival now stems from the churning sea of humanity, both internally and externally, with which it must cope.

How much and how fast have people changed? During the thirties my father struggled to provide the bare necessities for a family of eight children. His formal education was obtained in a one-room schoolhouse and was terminated at the end of the sixth grade. He never earned as much as today's legally required minimum. The company provided no vacations, sick leave, paid holidays, profit sharing, or pensions. The "bonus system" consisted of a Swiss clock or a turkey at Christmas.

My mother usually had the responsibility of managing a modest farm, with the children as her only source of labor. This endeavor was necessary in order to supplement my father's wages and provide most of the food for a growing family.

My father had no feeling of deprivation or made no requests for assistance from government agencies. He was very grateful for his job and the security it represented. He was loyal to the company and was more careful in caring for company property than his own. He never talked about job dissatisfaction—being bored, underpaid, or unfulfilled. Yet, over a lifetime of frugality and hard

11

work, he built a small estate. He seemed to have understood and accepted the purpose of his life.

My son, who is 26 years old and a college graduate, views life quite differently. He worked for a bank but felt unchallenged by the requirements of the daily system and was disenchanted with management's lack of idealism. Now he is in a commercial real estate partnership. He is willing to take the risks, accepting the consequences of success or failure. He wants the full and immediate rewards for his efforts. He wants the unstructured freedom to pursue opportunities. He is turned on and charged up by discovering, working out, selling, and successfully completing a major project. His lifestyle is largely of his own choosing. He wants to feel challenged and excited every day. He has worked on single projects that have already brought him more money than my father earned in a lifetime.

The world of my deceased father and my son are so vastly different that each might have great difficulty understanding the work ethic and lifestyle of the other. It would be difficult for my son to understand my father's daily drudgery and loyalty to a company that provided so little in return. My father would be perplexed by my son's need to be free to pursue courses of his own choice without the security of a regular salary.

THE HUMAN TRANSITION

The Forty-third American Assembly recognized the changing world of work and issued the following statement:

The world is caught up in cross currents of rapid change. Three distinct forces are involved: the institutions and jobs they provide, the society at large, and the individual worker. Each is changing at different rates of speed and with different degrees of responsiveness. The individual worker and the society are changing much faster than the institutions and the quality of jobs they provide.[1]

Gerald L. Phillippe, while chairman of General Electric, stated, "The greatest need is going to be for men who can manage change. This, we think, has become the first condition of leadership, not

[1] From "The Changing World of Work" Report of the Forty-Third American Assembly, November 1973, Harriman, N.Y., p. 4.

only in business, but in every other organized endeavor in our society." [2]

The rapid human change was characterized by Alvin Toffler as a "collision with tomorrow." [3] Command authority over people has been lost. This rather innocent fact has required major changes in the military, the Catholic church, and now in the operation of business enterprises. Loss of command authority leaves a vacuum —the inability to control behavior or to get things done through people. Response and action must now be attained on a merited, voluntary basis. This demands a totally different relationship and type of leadership. When people have the freedom to choose, they respond only when response is advantageous in meeting their needs and desires. Herein lies management's greatest challenge of the future—winning the business production battles with voluntary effort.

NEW DIMENSIONS IN THE HUMAN ERA

Fletcher Bryom, chairman of Koppers Company, writing in the February 1973 *Conference Board Record* stated:

I believe . . . that what happens between now and the year 2,000 may entitle this to be known as The Human Century. . . . There will be greater dignity in the work people do. . . . Early in this century a person could work full time and still earn no more than he needed to keep his family alive. Today, almost any person who works full time has discretionary income. . . . Technology has given people relief from the drudgery of work on a scale never before known. . . . As a result of a greater variety of opportunity, more and more of our people are achieving the state of self-actualization which the late psychologist and educator Abraham Maslow described as the highest level in the hierarchy of human needs. This involves the individual's recognition that he likes his job because it makes the best use of his abilities and because it represents his maximum contribution to society. Self-activity and the variety of opportunity that encourages it are best attained in a highly productive system.[4]

[2] Gerald L. Phillippe, "The Management of Change" *Proceedings 1967* American Association of Collegiate Schools of Business, St. Louis, Mo., 1967.
[3] Alvin Toffler, *Future Shock* (New York: Random House, 1970).
[4] Fletcher Byrom, "Conference Board Record," February 1973, pp. 2–4.

The following are some of the forces that are changing the mores of our society, our employees, our customers, and the general public.

Era of rapid transition. During certain periods in human history, there have been long spans of stability—relatively little change. Just the opposite appears true for the foreseeable future. The order of the day will be rapid and deep changes within a short time frame.

The death of permanence. Obsolescence is designed into products. Models and styles change annually. Fashion is seasonal and short-lived. The environment is one of planned obsolescence and change. We're in a throwaway society—paper clothing, disposable products, nonreturnable containers. The mood is one of mobility. Concepts and products are expected to pass rapidly into the outmoded era of the past.

Compressed lead time. Pendulums swing wider and more quickly. Cycles are shorter. Companies have less lead time to make model changes and correct errors when they occur. Employees believe that fulfillment of expectations can and should be achieved right now. The company must cope with compressed lead time in its people relations as well as in its products.

Exploding circle of communication and influence. In the past, isolated people with limited means of communication experienced very little influence from other people. Today, communication is worldwide and almost instantaneous.

We no longer have the advantage of dealing with isolated employees or customers. Their attitudes and their expectations are the result of a collective, wide-ranging influence. This has great impact on what the coal miner in Kentucky will accept. It shapes the motivation to which assemblers will respond in the General Motors plant. It dictates the nature of the relationship that must exist between executive and employee throughout the business community.

INCREASING HUMAN RESOURCE PRICE TAG

The total price tag for human resources constitutes one of management's key challenges. The combination of legislation, unions, competition, law of supply and demand, and rising expectations on the part of employees makes the rapidly increasing cost of time a major concern. The critical test is whether productivity can be increased as rapidly as the payroll to maintain an acceptable return on investment ratio.

At the Annual Conference of Human Resource Systems Users, sponsored by Information Science Incorporated, Dr. Eli Ginzberg, former chairman of the National Manpower Advisory Committee and one of the nation's leading human resource authorities, stated:

> Of all the resources that go into our economy and come out in income, something of the order of three-quarters are personnel-related costs. What more proof do you need that you ought to manage that resource better? For example, 54 percent or 55 percent (it varies from year to year) of the defense budget represents personnel costs. That's about $43 billion a year—talk about manpower problems! So I don't think that one need argue very hard that we must try to manage our human resources more effectively.[5]

The increasing uncertainty regarding human cost and availability and the complexity of ROI have set companies scurrying in all directions seeking substitutes for human effort. This has led to increased computerization and mechanization—in one company, three people managing and operating a giant electric-power-generating station; in another, one person at the electronic switch controlling an entire freight yard; and in the protection area one security guard before TV monitors handling security, gates, and movements throughout a vast plant.

Return on investment in human effort means streamlining all work processes, structuring the most efficient form of human organization, and redesigning jobs for maximum results. For example, electronic data processing is generally faster and more efficient, can process and retain more data, and can retrieve it more reliably than the human mind. The cost of human energy makes it necessary for management to use all forms of machine and electronic technology to make the use of human time more effective.

[5] Eli Ginzberg, "What Is the Future for Manpower Planning?" Reprinted in *The Computer & Human Resources,* March 31, 1975, prepared by Information Science, Inc., Montvale, N.J.

A LIMITED COMMODITY

A check of the classified section of any major Sunday newspaper reveals that the market for certain types of human talent is greater than the supply. Production falls behind and delivery schedules are cancelled for lack of employee contribution. Government and private groups seek to relocate labor supply to geographical areas of greatest need. Companies spend millions of dollars training and upgrading their own personnel to meet their needs. Aggressive and often expensive efforts must be made to attract and employ needed resources. This cost should lead to increased attention to short- and long-range planning for total human resources.

Human resources, viewed as a limited commodity, deserves special attention for maximum utilization. The company should make whatever adjustments are necessary to promote this goal. Current operation and future expansion are dependent on the availability of adequate human talent. (General economic recessions like the one that occurred from 1974 to 1975 exert only a temporary change on the availability of human resources. The trend after a recession continues in the same direction—human resources is a limited commodity.)

THE CHANGING HUMAN CLIMATE

It is probably too early to understand fully the magnitude of the changing human climate, but it is certainly too late to stem the tide. Older executives are inclined to bemoan the "erosion of what made the country what it is today," while younger employees will view the changes as the dawning of an exciting new era. But this reference to age might be misleading since attitudes, acceptance of change, and leadership of change are certainly not restricted to stereotyping based on age. Every age is caught up in the changing climate and is affected by it. Lifestyles are shifting and employees are ignoring old drummers and responding to a new rhythm. An examination of specific climate shifts spotlights the nature and extent of these changes.

A break with the past. Approximately one-half of the people living today are under age 30. They were born after World War II and have never lived through a depression. As the number of workers and executives who have experienced only affluence increases and the number shaped by scarcities and depressions decreases, significant changes will occur in the industrial climate. Employees will have a higher level of expectation and a different relationship with the company.

Changing composition of the workforce. Since World War II, over half of those added to industrial human resources have been women and blacks. This has necessitated changes in the physical work environment, types of supervision, employee benefits, and considerations for the legal consequences of all actions.

Increasing government control and benefits. More and more, government at all levels will exert control and impact on the human resources of a company. This influences who is employed and promoted, rates of pay, who will be trained, and types of supervision under which people will work. Every executive and every employee will have to understand the role of government in his or her work life. More than ever, employees will turn to government for benefits that they expect but might not otherwise receive from the company.

More options available to individuals. This means that people will have greater control over their lives and in turn that the company will be able to exercise less control. People will have greater options to leave their jobs, complain to the union or government, and disregard leadership directives. The creed will be that each individual is master of his or her own destiny and will not surrender this prerogative to any other individual or institution.

Shift from company to outside influence. The shortened workweek means that most employees will spend less than 15 percent of their lives at the workplace. The company will have less and less opportunity to shape the ambition, attitudes, work habits, and careers of its people.

CATALYSTS OF HUMAN CHANGE

Certain factors appear certain to alter our society permanently. These include the following.

Increasing educational attainment. More and more of the workforce will have finished high school, junior college, four years of college, and graduate school. Future policies and leadership must cater to better-educated, freer people. People will be smarter. Intelligent people expect to be free from ignorance, poverty, and hard physical work. This leads to less tolerance of anything they consider objectionable or unacceptable.

Shifting control of institutions. During the seventies, most institutions were under the control of leaders whose attitudes about "a day's work for a day's pay," gratitude for a job, respect for superiors, and acceptance of working conditions were shaped during the Depression years. Most of these presidents and top managers would have been in their impressionable early teens at that time. Company structure, policies, and creeds reflect the strong formative hand and continuing control of these conservatives. But the control of these institutions will shift rapidly to the control of people who are the products of post-World War II abundance. Fundamental policies regarding profits, social responsibility, treatment of people, and lifestyles will change accordingly.

Pressures to end the company system. It isn't necessary to trace industrial history back very far to discover that traditionally there was seldom any question regarding the difference between capital and labor or management and employees. The visibility was evident by the size and location of homes, clothing, forms of transportation, education of children, club and often church membership, and status within the company. This will no longer be true. Homes, clothing, education, automobiles, and golf club memberships will no longer distinguish owner and worker or be the direct reflection of a caste system within the company. This will make all individuals more equal in relationships and in fact.

THE EMERGING HUMAN PROFILE

What will employees and executives be like in the future? The most significant characteristics of the environment of our future human resource will be as follows.

A psychology of entitlement. Our society has raised the expectations of masses and individuals. Educators have led students to believe that increased education entitles them to more material rewards and a greater portion of the good life—instantly. Companies will have to be satisfied with getting less credit, gratitude, and hard work in return for fair pay and reasonable employee benefits. These benefits will be expected—every substantial company will have to provide them to be competitive, and the government will make them do it. Employees believe that results are possible, that changes can be made, and that the company can do the right thing if it really wants to.

A primary concern for personal fulfillment and gratification. Call it selfishness—because that is what it is—but personal fulfillment and gratification could be the most significant influence on the behavior of people. The individual will be less concerned with what the company wants. He or she will pay less attention to the Joneses. Each person will insist on doing his own thing, living his own life, working when and where he wants, and not letting work restrict weekend plans, vacations, and leisure activities. Each will insist on looking up from the grindstone and living life to the fullest his or her "one time around." And each individual will decide what this means.

A new criteria for success and work ethics. No one really has to kill himself working in order to enjoy a comfortable, affluent life. Americans are earning twice as much as they did 20 years ago, building better homes, buying more cars, taking more trips, sending their children to more camps, and more are living in air-conditioned houses and apartments. Although they have reached a general state of affluence, a strange uneasiness has occurred. A little more money, affluence, and material trappings have not solved as many "happiness" problems as anticipated. The disenchantment with big cars and expensive clothing is giving way to the natural life. There is an erosion of the traditional view that hard work always pays off. After work has provided the required economic benefits, it is then expected to provide psychological benefits.

The work ethic for the early pioneer was survival. For the unemployed of the thirties, it was hunger. But what is it today for a generation that has never been concerned with survival or hunger? Attitudes toward employment and work ethics are changing rapidly and have a direct bearing on work quality, employee turn-over, and labor unrest.

A growing sense of powerlessness and frustration. People have a deep-seated feeling of dissatisfaction. Things are happening that they don't like or approve. Government's wasteful programs and stifling regulations, the crumbling of traditional religious corner-stones, and the takeover of education by liberal long hairs constitute the thundering herd with which the individual experiences a sense of powerlessness to cope. They also experience a growing sense of powerlessness in trying to cope with bigness—big government, big business, big churches, and big universities. These unyielding institutions become the scapegoats for what really bothers people and for the more important things that aren't being changed.

The national paragons of law and order prove to be the most lawless, and some business executives profit at the expense of the unsuspecting. Why bite the proverbial bullet in the name of patriotism and cooperative brotherhood when the ripoff is tolerated and each person selfishly grabs for his or her share of the spoils of the "system"? If one cannot trust the FBI, whom can he or she trust? If a company leader can't be trusted, then what about the integrity of everything the company represents?

The result is suspicion, resentment, hostility, and lack of support. These negative feelings are often directed at the company when the individual fails to get the job, the promotion, the pay raise, and the career satisfaction that he or she feels entitled to.

Permissiveness in all areas and a feeling of an impending moral crisis. On the one hand there is a sanction of sexual permissiveness, divorce, abortion, use of alcohol and drugs, and free lifestyles. On the other hand, there is a sense of moral crisis, a fear that permissiveness is threatening the fabric of society. Crime, drug abuse, violence, and lack of integrity in government and business seem to be the norm. The hero of law and order turns out to be the bad guy in the person of the president and the vice-president of the nation. People become confused and anxious and do not know in what or in whom they can put their trust. The company and the boss are viewed with the same attitudes. The government is mistrusted and people want less and less interference from it in their lives, while at the same time they are—through pressure groups—demanding more services, handouts, guarantees, and protective laws.

IMPACT ON FORMS OF HUMAN ORGANIZATION

Organization charts and relationships will be less rigid and more fluid. The pyramidal (from the boss down) type of organization will give way to matrix, flat, free-form team structures. It will involve fewer company "thou shall nots" and "thou shalls." The organizational form will recognize a lack of absolute authority over others and will seek to create the structure and environment that will incorporate involvement, participation, and cooperative response. The attempt will be to create a climate that will develop and make maximum use of career aspirations, talent, creativity, effort, and personal life styles.

The form and nature of the organization will be in a constant state of flux. Individuals will have to learn to live with the uncertainties of changing duties and responsibilities. The situation will be what John W. Gardner has described as a consistently changing structure in response to the changing need—an ongoing process rather than a traumatic, once-in-a-lifetime affair.

CHALLENGES TO LEADERSHIP

Perhaps the most dramatic challenge to the company will be in the area of supervision and leadership. What effective practices can be substituted for loss of command authority and control over subordinates? The company now has to supervise, organize, and manage a workforce that is more permissive, will accept fewer rigid rules and policies, will insist on greater flexibility in work schedules and job assignments, will demand more options and voice in job decisions, will feel less obligation to the job and company, will be less grateful but will expect more, and will pose new challenges in the area of motivation.

As a result, there will have to be more tolerance of individual lifestyles and unconventional appearances. Employees will feel little loyalty to the company and its leaders, and there will have to be some tolerance of employee hostility—disagreement with the boss, strong voicing of a different point of view—and acceptance of continuing differences with a permanent state of personal coolness. Employees will insist on the full use of their talents, a direct benefit from their contributions, the opportunity to see the results of their efforts, and participation in decisions that affect their jobs. Their talents will have to be used more effectively. New forms of motivation must be discovered and implemented, probably through the redesign and enrichment of the work itself.

Leadership must develop new techniques and skills in order to cope effectively with the new human environment. Decisions, changes, and actions must be judged by their impact on people, and people in leadership will have to recognize that their actions will involve high risks—both legal and economic—as well as disruption and loss of productivity.

INFLUENCE OF LEGAL REQUIREMENTS

Legal requirements now constitute a major influence on what a company and its leaders at all levels can and cannot do. It is the company's responsibility to know the law and to see that it is followed.

Every supervisor, from first-line manager to president, is a legal agent for the company. His or her decisions and actions can have a major impact for the company. Overt acts, failure to act, or neglect of acceptable legal procedures can subject the company to a variety of charges, investigations, and additional costs. Serious concern must be given to a long list of complicated laws—many of which are given after-the-fact interpretation by government agencies and courts.

The more significant laws are those dealing with number of hours worked, overtime pay, executive exemptions, equal pay and opportunity between sexes and races, health, safety, social security benefits, unemployment, training, promotions, discharges, working conditions. These laws include the Fair Labor Standards Act, along with numerous amendments and interpretations; the Occupational Safety and Health Act; and the Equal Employment Opportunity Act.

The company has to make certain that everyone who interprets or takes action regarding these laws is thoroughly knowledgeable regarding their requirements. Periodic reviews must be made to see that all required posters are properly displayed. Company procedures, rules, guides, and programs must be checked and administered to ensure against violations. Written procedures must be made available to guarantee that there is no question regarding the company policy and how it is to be followed.

THE DRAMATIC UPHEAVAL

This chapter has been but a peek at perhaps the most dramatic upheaval in human attitude and organization restructuring in the history of mankind. Traditional mores and patterns within the industrial society have given way to new rules of the game. Dr. Daniel Yankelovich, educator and research psychologist, stated:

> Never have changes come so thick and fast and on every front. The economy is changing; the population mix in the country is changing; the political climate is changing . . . people are changing in complex ways that are difficult to understand, and yet, unless one understands the human side of the future, it's impossible to make sense of anything else. . . . There is a greater search for quality of life in the workplace, as well as the pursuit of leisure and tolerance of individual differences. There is less rigid acceptance of authority of any group . . . less personal prejudice against people who dress differently, think differently, or hold different points of view.[6]

In response to these shifting human patterns, company policies and leadership must show full recognition of people's needs by changing leadership styles and techniques to cope with increased education, accelerated expectations, and the exploding psychology of entitlement, by accepting the fact that people expect to be free from physical drudgery and insecurity. They must find ways to satisfy the wish for mobility through transfers, promotions, mid-career job changes, and company-initiated employee turnover.

Leadership must also respond to growing uneasiness, suspicion, mistrust, frustration, permissiveness, and the sense of moral crisis felt by employees, which will in some cases be in sharp defiance of our long-accepted work ethic.

The greatest concern should be to guard against underreacting or overreacting. Errors in either direction will result in missing the target.

[6] Speech before the National Retail Merchants Association, January 7, 1974, in New York.

GAUGING RESPONSE TO CHANGE

A word of caution must be given here. True, basic human expectations are undergoing vast change. We must learn from the past patterns of mankind but not be handicapped by them or our own experience. The previously successful guides to effective human relations should not be cast aside until better answers are available.

The American Assembly concluded its report on the "Changing World of Work" by stating:

> Something clearly is stirring. In part we are witnessing changes in personal values that are seen and felt not only in the United States but around the world. We are experiencing the latest chapter in the continuing story of the quest for fulfilling American Goals and aspirations: a fair and equitable society; an opportunity for each citizen to participate in the forces that affect his life; a confirmation that the democratic process does, indeed, work for all. Now that challenge is emerging at the most basic level of work itself. . . .[7]

The human challenges and relationships on the job will never be quite the same. But working with smarter, brighter, more individualistic, more ingenious, and more flexible people can be exciting and rewarding. Working with new forms of organization and levels of human resources promises new hope for better companies, better work environments, and more of the good life for everyone. Although the industrial human climate will never be the same, it has every potential for being better. Future results will depend largely on the response of management and society to vastly enlarged opportunities made possible through these human changes.

[7] "The Changing World of Work," Report of the Forty-Third American Assembly, November 1973, Harriman, N.Y., p. 10.

3
Achieving ROI
in human resources

A company president looked at the annual payroll budget and commented, "That's a lot of money to pay out when we can't be certain what we're going to get in return. I wish there were a way to measure return on investment in people as we do in other areas." An employee commented rather hopelessly, "Well, another year down the drain, and what have I got to show for it? I just don't feel that I'm getting anywhere. There ought to be some way to see where I've been, where I am, and where I'll be going in the future."

Both the company and its employees have reasonable aspirations—goals that should be mutually beneficial. As each party to the employment contract achieves its goals, it ensures the attainment of the goals of the other. They need each other and should be able to understand the interdependence of their needs and benefits. Human resource planning is an attempt to meet the legitimate needs of both the company and its employees.

The company's investment in human resources, payroll, benefits, and related costs involves the purchase of a rather unusual asset. It consists of "raw human time" and the uncertain contribution it will make. Once the purchase contract is made, the time and potential become available to the company. But the crucial question is, "What happens to this asset potential?" Whether this resource results in a return on investment will depend on whether the company sees that it is:

Properly trained.

Given effective leadership.

Given a physical environment conducive to productivity.

Stimulated to full effort.

Fully utilized through accurate matching of ability and job requirement.

Rewarded in proportion to contribution.

Retained and developed.

Given a reasonable opportunity to become involved.

The employee, for his part, must also make certain contributions beyond his mere presence before a return on investment can be expected, namely:

Commitment of time to full productive effort.

Response to training and development.

Response to opportunities for career growth through job enlargement and promotion.

Cooperation and linkage of work activities with those of others.

Mental and physical input that increases the asset value of the product, service, or process.

Both the company and the individual must make significant contributions before a return on their respective investments can be expected.

CONCERN FOR MAXIMUM RESULTS

The company and the individual should have genuine concern that each will receive the maximum return for his or her investment in the job-related arrangement. This vital benefit should not be left to hit-or-miss management. The large percentage of the company's operating budget, and the decisive impact of human resource activity, make this a priority concern. The individual should recognize that current success provides stepping-stones for future growth and that current failure jeopardizes future opportunity.

Both company and employee should deliberately seek methods, procedures, and programs that will provide the greatest assurance of mutual benefit. For the company, this must be a total, overall human resource program that provides both a short- and a long-range bottom-line return on investment in human resources. The individual must be able to recognize that his or her investment is with a company in which the system and the actual implementation of that system provide pay, opportunity, leadership, and job-related satisfactions in accordance with his or her needs.

ROI CONCEPTS AS PLANNING GUIDES

Roger Jauch and Michael Skigen state that, generally, we can all agree that employees are resources. However, they question whether employees can really be calculated as assets:

> Human resource accounting has been defined as the process of identifying, measuring, and communicating information about human resource to facilitate effective management within an organization. While no one denies that employees are a major factor in the future well-being of a firm, their valuation expressed in monetary terms is simply unworkable as a result of two factors. The first is the inability of the accounting profession to develop a meaningful system of measurement; and the second, which is of much greater theoretical importance, is that humans simply do not qualify as "assets" under the usual definition of the term—something of value owned by the firm. People are no longer owned.[1]

This point of view is acceptable from a strictly accounting standpoint, but from a practical operating position the company must use measurements for determining the relationship of investment in human resources to their contribution to the goals of the enterprise. This is the real purpose of the ROI in the human resource concept—an objective and hard-nosed, long-range evaluation of cost and return in the sizable people segment of the business.

A well-operated, profitable company should apply the return on investment test to its various operations, activities, and expenditures. If the purpose of the company is to achieve certain goals—volume increase, profits, cost control, and share of the market—it should be operated with an orientation toward the attainment of these goals. Ways must be found both to minimize waste of assets

[1] Roger Jauch and Michael Skigen, "Is Human Resource Accounting Really Practical?" *Management Review,* September 1974.

and to use them in the most advantageous manner to maximize results.

Typically, the ROI concept is applied to profit as a percent of total business volume. But the concern for ROI should be applied to evaluation of both financial and nonfinancial indicators. Financial indicators include earnings on sales, earnings per share, earning on equity, return on assets, return on invested capital, return on investment, sales growth, and capital investment.

The nonfinancial evaluation might include share of market, customer relations, new product or market development, and employee relations.

The results of company ROI evaluations should be checked against the individual employee's needs, which might include amount of pay and benefits, quality of management and direct supervision, opportunity for development, growth, and progress on the job, acceptability of the physical working environment, the employee's feeling about the job and the company, and the sense of total satisfaction and well-being he or she can achieve on the job.

Although financial, or money, management is the area in which return on investment is most often applied, money management also has to be concerned with planning and budgeting money requirements, plans for acquiring the money, developing ways for converting the money into an earning asset, ways in which all money assets are at work or are being fully utilized, programs to ensure that optimum use is being made of the asset, and a system for audit or control of the asset.

The return-on-investment concept in human resources must involve these same concerns; it should provide a planning and operating system to determine how much will be invested and when it will be invested, matching supply to needs, develop the asset for maximum utilization or contribution, measure asset contribution, bring about improved results, protect and enlarge asset value, and provide the assets needed for the continuity and growth of the company.

The return-on-investment concept applied to human resources provides a quantitative, integrated framework. If properly implemented, the plan should achieve a systematic, fair, mutually acceptable program, so that both the company and the individual will receive appropriate benefit from their investment.

IDENTIFYING ROI PREMISES AND DECISIONS

In proceeding with ROI in human resources, certain premises must be assumed and decisions made. There must be an assumption that the company has an ROI goal and that it has, or is willing to acquire (through internal development or outside sources), the expertise and skills necessary to structure and implement the system.

Human resource planning cannot occur in isolation; it must be supportive of and integrated into the total company planning process. Therefore if the company expects to engage in people planning, it must first engage in total company planning. Company goals and objectives must be established. Rate of growth and amount and types of change must be anticipated. An agreement must be made on what human resources will be needed and how much the company is willing to budget for this asset. Just as the company must make certain assumptions regarding the financial asset, it must also make certain assumptions about the human asset.

People-planning assumptions should reflect the creed or basic operating guides of the company. The assumptions and decisions should be legal, ethical, and fair. They should also build morale and team strength. They should provide a forward thrust toward all company goals. If the plan is to be implemented effectively, supportive decisions must be made.

HUMAN RESOURCE IMPERATIVES

Certain imperatives must be confronted and answered when focusing on the best solutions in the human resource area. Basic positions and priorities by management will determine what job is to be accomplished and how well the job will be done. The company's policies should be established and should cover:

The amount of money and percentage of total expenses allocated for human resource costs—principally payroll and benefits.

Promotions from within the company versus recruitment from the outside for jobs that would represent promotions and for which reasonably qualified candidates are available.

The resources that will be committed to training and development.

The importance of leadership as evidenced by the overall qualifications and effectiveness of supervisory management at all levels.

The assurances or guarantees given to individuals that their talents and full potential will be used to the fullest extent practical.

Loyalty, attitudes, motivation, and satisfaction of employees as a by-product of company action and communications.

The value the company places, by its decisions and practices, on human resources versus its other assets.

Company behavior will communicate to employees the nature of the organization and will ultimately determine their contribution to company goals. Employees will base their beliefs on company action, not on written creeds or policy booklets.

REPLACING BROMIDES AND PANACEAS

Never before have so many management consultants, behavioral scientists, social planners, educators, executives, government agencies, and special-interest groups offered so many, and such a variety of, solutions to the people puzzle. Beginning with early time-and-motion studies, and continuing to the present flood of panaceas, individuals and groups have marched onto the scene with patented prescriptions. Most solutions that have been advocated have been—at best—piecemeal, stopgap, and often experimental. They have often been expensive and occasionally disruptive to the stability of the employee group; they have at times seriously jeopardized jobs and normal operation.

This is not intended as a wholesale condemnation of the many worthwhile contributions made over the years by researchers and professionals. They have provided extremely valuable guides to management and have advanced the understanding of motivation, employee needs, and a variety of areas beneficial to employees. However, the caution flag is intended to remind management not to be taken in by unproved schemes, bromides, and pat answers to people problems. It just isn't that simple. Here are some of the techniques and plans that have flashed onto the stage in recent years: professional management, management by objectives, and participative management; sensitivity training, encounter groups, and transactional analysis; employee information systems, cafeteria compensation, human resource accounting, job enrichment, and conflict resolution.

Other methods we studied

The list could go on, an endless catalog of prescriptions meant to cure the human resource headaches faced by both management and employees. Millions of dollars have been invested in a variety of exotic programs, training sessions, workshops, printed material, and seminars. Additional millions have been spent for cassettes, video tapes, and other visual aids. Many of these have certainly made significant contributions, but many have been too complex and have required great expertise. Most managers are not doctors, scientists, or psychiatrists; yet they have attempted encounter sessions, participative management, and job enrichment and—on occasion—have experienced disastrous results and disillusionment.

It has been difficult for management to react to such programs. Questions have arisen, such as: Who can provide reliable guidance? What will the long-range effect be? Which should be implemented? Which should be rejected outright or modified? What is a reasonable cost in relation to the benefit? How should these programs be implemented? Assuming sincerity and willingness on the part of management to respond to these programs, there is still difficulty in making choices.

Management decision makers have become skeptical because the results that were promised failed to materialize. They have been led down false paths. They have generally learned that cut-rate quickies, bromides, and solutions cannot be relied upon to provide answers. Instead, the search is for better, more dependable, and longer-range solutions. The overall human resource concepts proposed in this book seek to provide the total foundation on which durable programs can be built.

TIME AND POTENTIAL AS THE RESOURCE

In focusing on the best solutions for a return on investment in human resources, the resource must be correctly understood. The resource in the context of this book is human time and potential contribution. Human resource planning and programs must therefore focus on the block of time purchased—a quantity resource—and an accurate evaluation of the potential contribution this time and talent can make toward meeting the goals of the company. Unless this key point is accepted, focus and programs will be concentrated in the wrong direction. If this happens, the ROI will fall back into the bromide-and-panacea ash heap. But if the steps advocated in subsequent chapters are properly implemented, a viable, productive human organization can be constructed.

4

Beneficiaries
of ROI
in human resources

Who are the beneficiaries of ROI in human resource planning? In order to justify its existence, every major company planning system should provide benefits—it should move a portion of the enterprise forward and give it a competitive advantage. The areas listed below are major beneficiaries of ROI human resource planning.

Financial

The fundamental purpose of the enterprise is served when financial goals are achieved. Financial effectiveness provides for dividends and reinvestment in the business, thereby making future growth possible.

Perhaps the best way to identify benefits of financial goal achievement is to examine the areas hurt most when the operation is financially unsuccessful. This list would certainly include stockholders, who would receive less dividend; employees, who might receive lower pay, fewer benefits, fewer promotions, and less opportunity to participate in developmental programs and who would experience less job security if the number of jobs should be decreased; customers, who might receive curtailed service and be denied the benefit of better products through various company research programs; and the general public, who might have to cope with the consequences of a failing business and reduction in the economic contribution the company is making. There would be a reduction of tax payments—which represent national defense, teacher salaries, police protection, medical research, and many other worthwhile government programs.

It would be difficult, if not impossible, to point out any area that would stand to benefit if the company were financially unsuccessful. All advantage seems to stem from companies that operate profitably and create the financial flow capable of providing benefits in many directions. It is the premise of this book that it is people who enable the company to make a profit. It is the type of advantage that only effective human resource planning makes possible.

Financial success results from the availability of qualified individuals who make the right decisions. The ROI concept should prevent the waste of human time and resource and its financial impact. The availability of trained, productive people, where needed, creates cash flow through the production and sale of goods and services. Appropriate leadership, working conditions, pay, and benefits make possible the retention of the vital human resource. The human resource plan provides specific steps for maximizing the productive benefit of individuals on the payroll, thus creating financial contribution to the company.

Appropriate human resource planning ensures that capable people are available to make profit. When financial and operating executives state, "Our people are our most important asset," they are completely accurate. They should also add, "Our people are our most important financial asset." The company's financial assets usually referred to are cash, securities, inventories, and physical resources. But Andrew Carnegie stated that if he lost all his financial and physical resources but could retain his people, he would be operating successfully again in short order.

Customers

The ultimate boss of every enterprise is its customers. The cash flow for its operation and continued existence comes from individual or institutional customers who are willing to buy the product or service being offered. Customers will take their business elsewhere if they are displeased. Although many utilities consumers do not have the freedom to purchase these services from alternate companies, they can retaliate by cutting back use when prices increase rapidly or service is unsatisfactory.

The success of the enterprise and its profitability are totally dependent on the opportunity for goal achievement represented by customer cash flow. Therefore, the best interests of the enterprise are served when it makes better products and services available to customers. In the trend to a system of management by objectives, one of the major goals should certainly be customer satisfaction and competitive superiority. What the company does internally should be secondary, with customer acceptance representing the ultimate and prime objective.

What do customers want? Specific answers will vary according to the product or service involved. The telephone caller wants the telephone to work. The client wants the lawyer to win the case. The patient wants to be cured. The car owner wants safety, reliability, and economy. The restaurant customer wants the food to taste good and to be available at reasonable cost. The airplane passenger wants to arrive safely. But regardless of the product or service, most customers have these common expectations:

A product that represents fair value for the cost involved.

A product that will perform the tasks claimed by the manufacturer and will last.

A product or service that is competitively priced.

A product on which service can be obtained if needed.

The opportunity to return the product for a refund or adjustment if not satisfactory or does not perform according to the manufacturer's claim.

Printed, and often personal, information supplied by the seller about the product and its use.

Reasonable courtesy, services such as credit and delivery, a safe, pleasant shopping environment, and a genuine effort on the part of the company to provide customer satisfaction.

Creditability—the opportunity of doing business with a company that is reliable; will make good on its promises; is honest in its claims, guarantees, and advertising; and exerts every reasonable effort to make things right when a complaint is made.

It is this type of customer satisfaction that provides the company with its profit opportunity. But how can the company be certain that this type of quality will consistently reach its customers? This is the role of human resource planning. When the plan is operated properly, the right people should be employed and trained. They should produce and deliver the type of products and services customers will find acceptable. When human resources are making the right decisions and producing effectively, it should be possible to deliver a product that is reliable and reasonably priced.

Customers, clients, patients, and patrons are principal beneficiaries of the ROI in human resource concept. It is based on having available high-quality, motivated, productive people to operate the enterprise. Their chief goals (even though from a standpoint of self-interest) should be the delivery of products and services that will warrant repeat business. Their attitudes toward the company, its leadership, their jobs, and what the company produces should cause employees to exert entrepreneurial effort to do their individual part in guaranteeing customer satisfaction. One textile manufacturing company kept this idea before its employees with the statement, "Remember that the customer is the next inspector."

The company stays in business only if it satisfies its customers. Customers will be satisfied only if they receive a product that is reliable, reasonable in price, and available through an acceptable process. The only way this can be accomplished by any enterprise is through its human resources. The ROI in human resource approach seeks to make available the type of people who are qualified and willing to engage in this type of job performance. If this is done well, it is the customer—along with the company and the individual employee—who benefits.

Employees

The highest form of human morality that can be practiced in a company is providing human dignity, status, career growth, reasonable compensation, appropriate leadership, and an opportunity to make maximum use of potential. Waste of human resources is management immorality. Perhaps it would be a reasonable analogy to compare the utilization of human resources with the Biblical parable of the talents. The human resource is the "talent" available to the company for the benefit of all concerned.

The individual benefits from ROI human resource planning by

knowing that he or she will be placed in a job most appropriate to his or her abilities and interests (depending on job availability) and that he or she will be trained to do the job in a satisfactory manner. The individual should have the assurance that he or she will receive constructive, humanistic leadership, will have an opportunity for job growth, and will be compensated fairly and that job security will be based on performance. The human resource plan should provide assurance to the individual that he or she will get from the job what he or she expects to receive.

Increasingly, individuals will have less willingness to become associated with or remain with a company that does not provide this assurance. The consistent operation of the human resource plan can be the best insurance the employee can have that he or she will receive this benefit.

Change, Growth, and Continuity

How can the company be assured that it will stay in business and that it will grow in the future? Perhaps no absolute guarantee can be given, but prudent companies do pursue those courses of action that provide the best potential for successful operation and growth. Products, markets, and procedures might change, but consistently successful companies anticipate these changes and take advantage of them. When the price of gasoline began rising, automobile manufacturers geared up to produce smaller economy models to compete with foreign-made cars. Motels were built to meet increased demands caused by more paid vacations and more leisure travel. Shopping centers were built to serve customers where and when they wanted to be served. Many downtown stores that did not go into the suburbs are now out of business.

Decisions that control the present operation of the business and shape its future are made by people—the human resources of the enterprise. Again it needs to be emphasized that human resources means all employees—from president to production worker. It is the quality of the human resource system that determines who will be making these decisions and who will be working to carry them out. These must be the types of decisions and efforts that provide for the effective operation of the company today, while at the same time assuring its future security and growth.

It can be assumed that when the human resource system has failed to make available people who make the right decisions and who engage in the right efforts, the continuity of the business will be jeopardized. However, when the human resource system does make available people who assure the success of the operation today and provide for its future growth, the short- and long-range interests of the enterprise are being served.

The Public and Society

The enterprise does not operate in isolation; it interacts with the society in which it exists. Also, it either benefits or damages that society by the nature of its operation. A profitable, growing company provides additional jobs, purchases more services, and contributes to the activities and projects of the community.

The local community, and society as a whole, benefits from company success produced by effective human resources. When a former president of General Motors said, "What's good for General Motors is good for America," he was making a reasonably accurate statement. But perhaps the statement would be more acceptable if it read, "What's good for America's free enterprise system, its economy, its ability to make jobs available, its capacity for paying dividends and taxes, and its production of goods and services benefits our total economic system." Too often, it is the abuses related to profit, pollution, or people that get all the attention. Companies that operate within the law, provide jobs, make a profit, engage in harmonious employee relations, and are good community citizens make little news. A classic example of this was the TV documentary "The Broken Promise," concerning abuses by a few companies regarding private pension programs. The one-hour program highlighted isolated instances of the worst type of abuse. No attention was given to the thousands of pension programs that are well founded and operate in the most creditable manner. Only at the end of the program was a postscript-type statement made that the abuses shown throughout the program were not necessarily true regarding all pension programs.

HUMAN RESOURCE PLANNING BENEFITS EVERYONE

Companies that are operated by competent human resources create an ongoing enterprise that makes a significant, far-reaching contribution to employees, customers, and society. The quality of what it does enhances or diminishes faith and confidence in the system of production and distribution. Governments are toppled when the system fails to provide jobs, food, and confidence. The health and continuity of the American system depend on its ability to operate effectively in providing the basics on which the system depends—jobs, production, distribution, services, and finance.

It is the human resources within the individual enterprise and the total system that determine the company's degree of success. Human resources within companies that ensure effective operations are also providing a vital benefit to the total American system.

5
Planning
a system for
total ROI

ROI in human resources is far more than a manpower replacement schedule. It involves the basic philosophy, attitudes, practices, utilization, and opportunities regarding the people of an organization. The profit squeeze, increasing size, and complexity of organizations have demanded closer attention to people costs and problems. These have forced a serious reassessment of human resource management. Eli Ginzberg emphasized "there is still a very wide gap between the experience of most corporations when it comes to financial planning, inventory planning, marketing planning, facilities planning, and this new baby called manpower planning." [1]

Business and industrial planning has traditionally focused on profit, production, finance, marketing, and inventory. Only recently has serious attention been given to human resources. As long as there was an oversupply of labor and minimal skills were required, training time was short and labor cost was low; companies could afford to disregard human resource planning. When temporary

[1] Eli Ginzberg from "What Is the Future of Manpower Planning?" Speech before the Fifth Annual Conference of Human Resource Systems Users. Reprinted in *The Computer & Human Resources,* March 31, 1975, prepared by Information Science, Inc., Montvale, N.J.

shortages occurred, emergency attention was given to a form of manpower planning, but as soon as the fire was extinguished, people planning was shelved.

Since World War II, people and skill shortages have often been the control factors limiting company growth. Launching of certain projects never materialized because the necessary personnel were unavailable. Also, the rapidly increased cost and expectations of employees have forced management to focus more attention on this key company influence. Additional commitment is now being given to training and development as a means of increasing productivity and ensuring a greater return on payroll investments. Progressive companies have begun making advance plans for replacements, anticipating manpower needs, and integrating these with training and related costs. But it has been difficult to measure and justify the cost of various human resource programs. Economy drives have caused manpower plans to be neglected or scrapped entirely.

In many instances, the plans were not professionally designed and the results were disappointing. The company as a whole seemed relieved when it could abandon "do-gooder schemes for more important work." But gradually the scores came in; the companies with the best profit and growth rate were also the companies with the best human resource plans. Companies that had anticipated their human needs as to numbers and skills could expand and take advantage of opportunities as they became available. There was overwhelming proof that anticipatory planning regarding people is not an expensive frill; rather, it is the key to achievement in all other areas. Advanced planning proved more economical and effective than emergency solutions. It became evident that people planning, as well as financial planning, could not occur isolated from all other areas of the company. Gradually, more enlightened companies not only provided human resource planning but also elevated this function to top management rank and made it an integral part of the total planning process. The cost of human time, the expectations of employees, and the legal risks involved persuaded management that people concerns could not be left to chance.

MANPOWER PLANNING VERSUS
HUMAN RESOURCE PLANNING

Traditional manpower planning is defined loosely as the process by which an organization ensures that it has the right number of people, with the right kinds of qualifications, at the right places, and at the times when they can be most economically utilized. Implementing the requirements of this definition involves:

—Replacement planning as related to personnel recruitment policies, analysis of labor turnover, career planning, promotional policies, and the relationship of pay and benefits to the employment and retention of people.

—Staff personnel administration functions as related to recruitment, selection, placement, training, development, labor relations, safety, and the administration of employee benefits, wages, and salaries.

—Manpower supply as affected by the economy, available supply of numbers and skills, cost of acquiring and maintaining an adequate supply, and projections necessary for meeting these goals.

The concept of human resource planning in this book is vastly different from the traditional forms of manpower planning. Manpower planning has typically been confined to providing for a supply of employees as replacements or to meeting increased needs. It usually dealt with numbers of people and, sometimes, with qualifications and training. It was generally low key and was limited to a staff function.

Human resource planning, if properly executed, involves every phase of the company. First, it must translate company plans into human resource requirements. It evaluates the current performance levels of individuals and predicts their potential. It must provide for career management or charting, and provide systems, forms, guides, and charts for matching job requirements with skills available. There must be feedback, evaluation, and recycling of the human planning process so that the individual's contribution can be measured as a return on human investment.

Finally, human resource planning encompasses everything that involves and concerns people—cost, morale, leadership, productivity, forms of compensation, and conservation of the resource. Fully implemented, human resource planning involves new dimensions and approaches to people planning. It provides for the total human input required by the company and assures a planned return for this cost.

BASIC APPROACHES TO HUMAN RESOURCE PLANNING

The approach to human resource planning should:

Assist the company and each operating unit in meeting their profit, growth, and operating objectives through planning for the effective, economical use of human resources.

Identify human resource needs for the total organization and initiate plans to meet them.

Prepare for the productivity, growth, and development of people.

Provide systems and procedures that will maximize the utilization of human time and potential.

Furnish the environment necessary to attract and retain productive people.

This concept places human resource planning where it belongs —in a supportive role that enables all other functions to achieve their goals. This can be accomplished only by anticipating future patterns of the organization, by defining the skills and qualifications of people at all levels in the present and future organization, and by deciding the most likely place to find people with required skills. Then realistic plans for the necessary development and/or recruitment of such people must be outlined, which means the systems, programs, and human resource data management that will make it possible for employees to move and grow through promotions, transfers, and job design. The basic approach to human resource planning must focus on providing that input or contribution that the human element must make to the enterprise in order for all other functions to operate successfully. This must be done at an acceptable cost and with minimum disruption. This approach should, at appropriate stages, involve the entire company—not just a few isolated planners. It eventually becomes involved with everything in the company, from compensation and communications, to product and marketing decisions.

IDENTIFICATION OF HUMAN RESOURCE COSTS

One of the problems associated with human resource accounting is the difficulty of identifying costs and measuring results. It is simpler to identify the cost of raw materials or advertising. Most planning forms and reports deal with financial or non-people data. When the president of a major bank was asked how much the bank spent for human resources, he pulled the annual report from his desk and pointed to the payroll cost. He observed that his bank's expenditure for employees seemed to be in line and that he wasn't too worried about it. Both the annual report and the president failed to include the many human resource costs associated with training, employment, employee benefits, and employee turnover.

The first valid step in providing for a return on investment in human resources is the identification and inclusion of all of the expenses involved. What expenses should be included? What are the types and amounts that must be a part of a true accounting procedure? As a start, these costs should be included:

Direct payroll and company contribution to Social Security.

Cost of all pay for time not worked—vacations, sick leave, and the like.

Direct and indirect cost of the portion of all employee benefits that involves a cost to the company.

People-related facilities and services—cafeterias, employee parking, lounges, lockers, and uniforms.

Financial services—credit unions, assistance with budgeting and taxes.

Medical and health-related services—first-aid personnel, supplies, rooms, equipment, facilities, and outside services.

Expenses of personnel administration—personnel for providing the services, supplies, equipment, and space; reference checking, recruiting ads and efforts; and related services.

Employee social and recreational activities—sponsorship of bowling teams, employee parties, and events involving employees and/or their families.

Training and development and various types of improvement programs—internal and those sponsored outside.

Costs involved in discounted products or services to employees.

Costs involved in complying with government regulations that relate principally to people—Occupational Safety and Health Act, noise control, air purification, reports, and cost of personnel to administer various government-required programs.

Payments for unemployment compensation insurance, workmen's compensation, and related taxes.

Child-care services and educational grants to employees' children.

The list could be continued and would vary according to employee services and facilities provided by each company. The total cost for all these expenditures often amounts to 70 percent of total operating expenses. This is the amount the company must pay to purchase the employees' time and to be reasonably certain of their presence on the job.

Some of these costs are specifically required by law—contribution to Social Security, unemployment compensation insurance, safety, and some employee facilities. Some are negotiated and specified by union contract. But the majority are furnished voluntarily by the company. These benefits are provided in some instances simply because the company recognizes the reasonableness and desirability of doing so. Many are supplied so that the company may remain competitive. Some benefits involve service, forms of security, and types of group insurance on which the company can obtain a cheaper rate than that available to individuals. Others, such as child-care services, transportation, and health care, are designed to ensure the employee's availability for work.

If the company is to be concerned with a return on investment in human resources, the amount of that investment must be computed. Failure to identify and include all costs related to the purchase of time constitutes the principal fault in most accounting for return on investment in human resources.

Few companies have ever made a serious attempt to calculate the actual cost of human resources. The limited efforts that are made often involve only the more obvious costs of payroll and employee benefits. Strangely, many companies take the attitude, "We're not certain how much it is, but we know it's too much and the cost is increasing rapidly. If we knew the amount, we'd probably decide we couldn't afford it. Maybe it's better that we don't know—one less thing to worry about!" But the fact remains that this expense involves the largest percentage of total operating costs, and in most instances involves the most avoidable waste of money.

PLANNED AND CONTROLLED
HUMAN RESOURCE PURCHASES

Planning for and controlling human resource purchases involve not only employment and hours worked but also all the expenses in connection with the purchase of that time. Planning must include and answer:

1. What human resources will be purchased?
2. Which cost-related services and facilities will be provided?
3. How much will be paid for the various items?
4. What percentage of total costs can the company afford to pay for human time?
5. How can resources, facilities, and services be made available in the most efficient and economical manner?
6. How can the availability of human time and related costs best be planned for, budgeted, and controlled within acceptable limits?
7. What possible cost can be avoided as it might relate to the purchase of human time, compensation and benefit systems, organization structure, training, and supervision?

The key steps in this process are deciding what the company wants to provide or purchase, establishing cost, developing an overall plan, and establishing controls and checkpoints to ensure that the plan is being followed and that expected objectives are being reached. Acceptable results depend on logical, complete planning to the same extent that a house reflects the blueprints. What happens, the amount of money spent, and the activities engaged in should be the result of an overall plan and not of helter-skelter decisions based on responses to situations. Human resource planning and control involve the most prudent use of dollars and human time and thus assure the greatest benefit to the company and the employee.

SPECIFIC HUMAN RESOURCE PLANNING GOALS

Human resources, like financial resources, must have specific goals. Planning and expenditures should be oriented toward those goals. The human resource planning goal should be to make available, at an acceptable cost, the human contribution necessary for the company to reach its various profit and operating goals.

From these general goals, specific and manageable goals must be developed. The question is, "Which specific resource goals must be met in order to reach the overall company goal?" They might include:

Goals and standards for availability of replacements. Replacements will be available for 90 percent of the jobs at least 45 days before needed. Most professionally managed companies set specific replacement goals as to time and qualifications.

Percentage of promotions that should occur each year. At least 20 percent of all employees will be promoted or experience some form of job enlargement. This meets the goal of promotion from within and that of constant people growth.

Number of people involved and types of training and development. At least 90 percent of all employees will be engaged in some form of training. This assures that most people will be growing and improving.

Employee turnover goals. Turnover will not exceed 15 percent for the year. This forces attention on control of employee turnover.

Specifics for evaluation of job performance. Job performance reviews will be conducted for 95 percent of all jobs. These reviews will provide evaluation for purposes of pay, promotion, and development.

Cost limits on payroll and employee benefits. Such costs will not exceed 68 percent of total operating budget of the company. This sets a specific limit on the dollar cost.

Goals for training supervision. Each year 90 percent of all supervisors will engage in formal training designed to improve leadership skills. This should assure the availability of both the quantity and the quality of leadership desired.

Measurement and improvement of productivity levels. Productivity will be monitored and increased at least 5 percent. This goal provides for measuring and improving productivity.

Communication of employee benefits. This focuses employees' attention on the cost of benefits and their advantages.

Opportunity for job performance review. Employees will be assured of a job performance review and an interview with their supervisors at least once during the year. This lets employees know where they stand, the company's evaluation of their contribution, and what they can do to enhance their opportunities for the future.

The human resource function must be oriented around specific, quantified goals and standards. These should include numbers, dollars, percentages, maximums, minimums, dates, amount of time, and the specifics that can be planned for, communicated, measured, and eventually evaluated when the target date has been reached. Areas in which this function operates are planned dollar and percentage cost, maximum utilization of the human resources purchased, an acceptable ROI for the company, and maximum benefits and opportunities for the individual.

PLANNING BASED ON RESOURCES AND PRIORITIES

Human resource planning should always be oriented toward achieving company goals. The purpose of the company is not to plan for or to provide human resources but to reach profit goals based on the primary activities of the company (in most instances, some form of production, sales, or services). Making human resources available should enable the company to reach these goals. In this process, if proper planning and execution are occurring, individual needs and goals will also be met. In addition, the company should be rendering important economic and community services. Thus in planning for human resources and related activities, decisions and priorities should be oriented around these primary company goals. Specific human resource goals that are supportive to company goals must be established and reached.

The activities that must occur if these goals are to be met must be integrated into the human resource plan. These include employment, promotions and transfers, training and development, proper forms of compensation; the assurance of constructive leadership, and the various other activities that must be part of the overall plan. The plan should also identify the decisions that need to be made in the implementation process. The advantage of forward planning is that provision will be made for the inclusion and coordination of all activities that must occur. But even in a well-constructed and well-implemented plan, priorities must be set. These include making certain that all positions are filled, insuring that all plans, decisions, and actions are legal, and making provisions for the communication of all intended decisions and action. Attention must be paid to avoiding or minimizing negative consequences on employee relations (morale, turnover, union contracts, and human climate). Provisions should be made for testing the impact on production and overall goal efforts of the entire company, and there must be planning for contingencies and alternatives.

Planning must ensure that needed human resources will be available from the standpoint of both quantity and quality. It must also ensure that necessary decisions are being made, that activities are occurring, and that priorities are being adhered to in moving toward the accomplishment of company and employee goals.

STEPS IN HUMAN RESOURCE PLANNING

A prerequisite of human resource planning is the availability of certain basic personnel information. This would include individual employee demographic and related employment background factors such as age, education, sex, work history, length of service in the organization, and other personal information. It must also be assumed, as a basis for human resource planning, that there exists a system of wage and salary administration and job evaluation. It must also be assumed that a system is available for collecting, systematizing, and retrieving the information needed for purposes of human resource planning and decision making.

Although there is no set formula or pattern that must be followed in human resource planning, the following are the basic steps.

Establishing the need for human resources. This step in the planning process should identify the current and future needs for human resources. Included must be all the processes that must occur in order to determine these needs. This becomes the basis for all other people-related activities.

Inventory and evaluation of resources available and/or to be acquired from outside sources. Once the need has been established in step 1, the next step is determining how these needs will be met. This involves inventorying the number and qualifications of present employees and forecasting their future potential to identify any existing gaps that will have to be filled from other sources.

Training and development to meet current and future goals. What will happen to purchased human resources? Will they be trained and developed to ensure the attainment of present and future goals? This is basically the role of training and development, which should focus on qualifications and performance needed to meet human resource goals and should seek to enlarge the potential of individuals so that requirements will be realized.

Maximum utilization of human resources. This step involves placement, accurate matching of qualifications and jobs, transfers, promotions, restructuring of jobs, all areas of productivity, leadership, forms of human organization, and the influences that impact on the effective use of human resources. This is probably the most neglected step in attempts to achieve a return on investment in a human resource program.

Provision for compensation, benefits, motivation, and retention of resources. It can be correctly stated, "We should never pay people in money alone." Other job-related needs, such as recognition, a sense of accomplishment, and self-satisfaction, must also be met. But the intangibles will not substitute for appropriate compensation and employee benefits. Human resource planning involves specific provisions for compensation, benefits, motivation, and retention of the resource.

Motivation should be a joint effort on the part of the company and the individual—both benefit. The employee who is producing more, is making career progress, and is responding fully to job-related opportunities will, at the same time, be receiving more of what he or she wants from the job.

ORGANIZING FOR HUMAN RESOURCE PLANNING AND UTILIZATION

The organizing process for implementing ROI in human resource concepts follows basic professional management guides.

The plan should make provision for certain things to happen and for the resources to make them occur. The plan should cover:

Who is responsible? Who will be assigned the responsibility and accountability for human resource planning and implementation?

What resources will be made available? The plan should provide for budgets, personnel, office space, and other required factors.

What data will be used? Provision should be made for access to all company planning, goals, contemplated changes, and individuals who are in a position to provide information.

What dates, deadlines, and time frames will be set? Other company plans, operations, and goals involve timing and time goals. Organization for implementing human resource programs must be equally precise and disciplined in order to make their required contribution.

How will the decisions, activities, and plans be integrated with all other company processes? Human resource activity should never be isolated. It must be integrated with and supportive of all primary company functions.

The rapid rise in emphasis on human resource planning has been responsible for the title "human resource specialist." Other titles for this function are vice-president, human resources; human resources director; manpower specialist; human resources planning director; or variations of the human resource manager concept. Regardless of the title, this individual or office must have an effective working knowledge of the organizational structure and policies, skills in planning techniques and control and implementation, and effectiveness in persuading managers at all levels to support and carry out these plans. Also necessary would be knowledge regarding various educational and training techniques, the ability to serve as a spokesman regarding internal human resource matters both within and outside the company, the ability to interpret government regulations and to comply with the legislation relating to human resources, and the ability to formulate effective and acceptable policies for dealing with various areas of human resources.

Planning and organizing for a return on investment in human resources must be a total approach. The principal cause for failures is a piecemeal, fire-fighting system. All too often, management fails to recognize the importance of ROI, fails to become involved personally, and fails to provide adequate budgets and facilities for its achievement. Executives—and often human resource professionals—have prescribed aspirins while ignoring serious symptoms and the need for corrective solutions. Human resources, which consume the greater part of the company's expense dollars, determine what the company achieves today, whether it will continue to exist, and what it will be tomorrow. This certainly merits the attention and supportive action from all levels of management necessary to ensure its success.

6

Steps in determining human resource needs

For many companies, strange and unexpected things happen on the way to the future. These organizations suddenly discover gaping holes in their needs for people and skills. Costly emergency outside recruitment follows. At other times large surpluses occur, necessitating expensive layoffs to pare employees down to affordable levels. People must be transferred to locations where needed. Improper balances of numbers and skills almost always result in additional expenses, delays, and disruption in the work activity. There should be a better way—and there is! The solution is an accurate determination of current and future needs for people and skills. When this assessment takes place, there is ample opportunity for meeting any needs that might occur.

Exxon's program for determining needs is closely coordinated with the company's business plan. Each division manager must draw up a long-range plan for the needs of that division and steps to be taken to meet these needs. A part of this requirement is appraising all key managers, forecasting job openings for the following five years, and assessing the most likely candidates to fill them.

A manufacturing plant in Virginia limits identification of needs and replacements for the local plant up to the foreman level. Since it is considered impractical to relocate employees below this level, companywide human resource planning beyond each plant is from this level up.

A New York bank identifies needs by management levels

within each branch and throughout the entire company. Although specific systems and procedures vary, the goal is to identify present and future human resource needs in sufficient time to meet the needs through planning.

DEFINING THE FUTURE

Analysis of the future, or inventing relevant futures, is fraught with risk and uncertainty. But a deliberate, conceptual consideration of known and predictable events provides the best procedure available for deciding what the future will be. If the process takes into consideration trends, operating environment, and what the company hopes to become in the future, planning can be amazingly accurate.

Many company decisions must be made years in advance—an atomic-power-generating plant requires ten years for approval and construction. Major steel plants require five years from decision to build to date of operation. A large department store requires three to five years from initial planning to opening day. Once these basic decisions are made, human resource needs can be identified for a specific future time.

Companies periodically redefine the nature of their businesses and, depending on the type of business, make projections three, five, and ten years into the future. The annual operating plan becomes a one-year projection. Almost every plan the company makes involves changes that in some way will affect its human resource requirements. Future operations must be financed and they must be staffed. Capital needs can often be met, depending on the current money market, more quickly than human needs. It takes time to locate and train people. Lead time becomes very important in making people and skills available at the time needed. Making these available in the right place and at the right time is a primary goal of human resource planning. If done properly, a successful plan can provide significant benefit in terms of reduced personnel costs, reduced recruitment costs, increased productivity, and longer retention of the existing workforce.

Forecasting human resource needs involves far more than counting heads. It involves examining and interpreting what company plans mean in terms of people. It involves taking variables, uncertainties, options and unforeseeable changes and molding them into a viable human resource plan. It means structuring alternates into the plan and requires flexibility for changing direction, recycling, and coming up with a new plan. Skeptics often argue that planning for the future is useless since it is impossible to tell what the future will be like. The truth of this belief must be admitted, but planning for what represents the best available facts about the future, and what the company plans to make happen, is preferable to vacuums and emergencies. Viable planning should always make provision for the constant updating and rolling forward of premises and results. If operating projections are over or under target, numbers of positions will be affected.

NEEDS BASED ON QUANTITATIVE GOALS

The whole foundation of realistic human resource planning is based on company needs. But how will these needs be determined? What are the present requirements for human resources—numbers and skills—and what will these be at various stages in the future? The present can be reasonably determined, but what will future predictions be based upon? Guesses? Wishful thinking? A straight-line projection of the past? An over- or underreaction to compensate for past errors?

Company planning and human resource planning are inseparable. Establishing human resource needs is simply a process of translating corporate objectives relating to present and future operational plans into numbers and types of jobs required. People planning must be based on the specific quantitative goals of the company. Specific numbers must be available regarding quantity, quality, time and dates, and cost; for example,

How much does the company plan to produce and sell at certain stages in the future?

How well does the company expect to operate regarding profits, expense margins, and quality control?

How much time will be allocated to reach certain goals, and what will be expected by certain dates?

How much will the company allocate in dollars and percentages for achievement by certain stages?

How many people will be needed to implement plans and achieve results?

Planning must be based on dollars, percentages, dates, and specific company objectives. Human resources, its decisions, and its mental and physical contribution will enable the company to reach these goals. Their attainment is dependent on this input at appropriate times and in proper amounts. Lacking this, goal achievement will suffer.

Human resource needs are derived from an analysis of people needed to implement and achieve total company plans. The purpose is not pooling or building a backlog of people but, rather, making them available as needed. Attempts to inflate or underestimate needs can be costly and disruptive to company goals. Inaccurate projection of skill requirements can cause delays, inadequate performance, or high-cost acquisition from outside sources. The key to human resource planning is the determination of needs, based on and linked as precisely as possible to, the specific plans and goals of the company.

IDENTIFYING CURRENT AND FUTURE PATTERNS OF ORGANIZATION

Accuracy and reliability in identifying future patterns of the company are critical ingredients in establishing needs. The following checklist can serve as a guide in deciding what the organization might be like in the future:

What new facilities will be put into operation?
What existing facilities will be closed?
To what extent will existing facilities be expanded or reduced?
What changes will be made in layers of management and organizational structure?
To what extent will qualifications for existing positions change?
What new positions and qualifications will be created and which ones eliminated?
What new products, machines, techniques, processes, and company locations will be added or reduced?
How many positions will exist at each level and in each category?

What skill and performance level will be required for each
position?
What positions exist now, and on what dates in the future will
others have to be filled?

It is easy to recognize the difficulty of answering these questions accurately. The process is concerned with examining past
trends and current development and then constructing a working
model of the system or body of data. This, in conjunction with
what can be anticipated about future trends, directions, planned
changes, and variables, becomes the basis for assumptions about
the future. This means taking what is known about the past and
projecting the same trends into the future.

The fundamental human resource determination must be one
of numbers and types of positions that exist or will exist in the future. Company plans, goals, and methods should provide this
information.

ANTICIPATING CHANGES

Considerable skill and value judgment must be exercised in
evaluating the impact of company changes on human resource
requirements. What impact will changes have regarding more or
fewer jobs? What skills will become obsolete, which changed in
nature, and which eliminated?

What trend is the company experiencing currently? What is its
record of change and growth? Can the company realistically expect to implement its plans and reach its goals? Are the assumptions on which planning is based factually documented and realistic regarding all human elements? Can the company finance the
facilities necessary? Are share-of-the-market and growth projections realistic? Human resource forecasts, based on faulty assumptions or unrealistic expectations, must inevitably fail. It isn't always
appropriate for the human resource planners to pass judgment on
projections or to question company plans, but often clarifications
of the need for people and skills provide testing and verification of
these projections.

Anticipated changes focus attention on the impact of these
changes on human resource needs. The current trend to fewer
layers of management could eliminate some existing or planned

management positions. Job enrichment, or enlargement—each position being given larger amounts of responsibility—could change the number and qualifications for certain positions. Innovations in technology, mechanization, and electronics could both eliminate and create jobs and skills. The company's projected growth in production and sales might be accomplished with fewer people instead of more. Streamlined processes, new breakthroughs in techniques, pre-processed raw materials, new forms of advertising, realignment of sales territories, and setting of higher quotas could provide clues regarding human resource needs.

The availability of a reliable human resource supply when currently needed should make allowance for turnover and absenteeism, and for individuals who fail to reach necessary production levels. A judgment, based on experience, might have to be made that a certain overage of positions must be provided in order to have adequate performance occurring at all times. This is analogous to a retailer's providing enough inventory to reach sales goals by making allowances for shrinkage caused by shoplifting and other reductions of retail value.

Determination of needs should be sufficiently flexible to permit the quick implementation of options. Contingency plans should be available. There must be quick human resource reaction if the company suddenly makes a decision to change direction, add new products or services, divest itself of certain divisions or units, or develop company plans that would require the complete revamping of the human resource plan.

Various legal requirements, government inspections, executive orders, affirmative action programs, safety measures, and outside pressures often have drastic and sudden implications for human resource planning. Positions have had to be created for disadvantaged persons, women, blacks, and other minorities. This has occasionally involved deadlines and numbers. This outside influence not only has caused the creation of new positions but also has brought about the elimination of others. Higher wage rates have influenced the trend to fewer people who can assume more responsibility. The equal pay requirement has eliminated many lower-paying jobs traditionally occupied by women and blacks. When these employees are paid more, available payroll dollars are shared among fewer positions.

Forecasting the changes and need for people is, at best, complex and hazardous. But it is the substance on which numbers, types of positions, and target dates must be built.

USING ALL SOURCES OF PLANNING DATA

All available data and all sources of information should be used in determining human resource needs. Every piece of information, inside and outside the organization, that might conceivably have influence on the company and its need for people should be considered. Sources of data should include:

—All company plans, objectives, and goals.
—Meetings with people who are in a position to influence the company future.
—Lists of all identified changes and their impact on human resource needs.
—Costs and trends of payroll and employee benefits.
—Analysis of present positions and skills to determine what changes should be made regarding current need for people.
—Forecasts for each area of the company by top management and leadership at every level.
—Government, national, and local influences.
—Financial and facility plans as indicative of need for people.
—Files, forecasts, and other types of information available throughout the company.
—Projected influences of changes in organizational structure and technology.

The more thoroughly all sources of influence are taken into consideration, the more likely it is that the final plan will be realistic and will represent actual resource requirements. Persistent, tenacious effort must be made to seek out all sources of information, to analyze the data, and to make an accurate judgment regarding its impact on the need for people and skills.

LISTING THE QUALIFICATIONS NEEDED

Eventually, all human planning needs should be reduced to numbers. This first step involves only the establishment of the number of positions and the types of qualifications needed; it does not consider the availability of people or the manner in which these positions will be filled. These requirements should basically include (1) the total number of positions, (2) the number of positions in each identifiable job classification, (3) a position description for each significant classification, (4) a listing of key qualifications and skills required for each classification, often called job specification, (5) whether the job will be permanent or temporary, and for how long, if temporary, and (6) where the job will be located. These requirements should be systematized in such a manner that they can be used for the next planning step.

ESTABLISHING DEADLINES

The final step in scheduling needs should include dates and deadlines. Existing positions that are not expected to change in number or qualifications should be treated as continuously filled. Specific times and dates should be placed by each position change. Changes and needs should be scheduled as close to the action date as practical. The date on which the position must begin making a productive contribution should be established. The required lead time should be set. If a new plant is scheduled to open on January 1 two years hence, then a determination should be made regarding dates on which the various positions will be filled. If a branch bank will open in 90 days, a decision should be made regarding when individuals will be employed or transferred into each position.

The key date is the time at which the position must be making a scheduled contribution. Establishing dates for the beginning of these positions involves backtracking to determine how long it might take to recruit, train, locate, transfer, or otherwise fill the position in order that it make the contribution according to schedule.

In planning for human resource needs certain forms and guides for gathering and recording information should be used. The information should be stored in such a manner that it can be used for required additional planning stages. Provision should be made for constant revision and updating of the final number and qualifications. Forms and guides used for this purpose are often available from publishing houses and other sources. The general procedure

Figure 1. *Forecasts of manager/manpower requirements.*

	Rationale of Needs	Forecasts of Manpower Needs			
		19 ___	19 ___	19 ___	19 ___
Top Management					
Middle Management					
First-Line Supervisors					
Second-Line Supervisors					
Labor					
Skilled					
Unskilled					

Source: Lloyd J. Hughlett, "Long-Range Planning Implemented by Management by Objectives" (Boone, N. C.: Executive Resources Development Institute, Inc.).

is to analyze forms used by others as guides and then construct new forms to meet the special needs of the company. Some people make serious mistakes in attempting to use unchanged forms and guides that might be the perfect pattern for another company but not for their own. Each company is different and has its own special input and needs.

Figure 1 is a form for recording forecasts of manager/manpower requirements. It focuses human resource planning processes on specific positions, need justification, and dates. This total look makes possible an analysis of position relationships, promotions, transfers, and the required timing frame. Once this form has been completed, it can serve as the planning base for the needed development, mobility, and acquisition of human resources.

Steps in determining human resource needs become the foundation on which all other human resource planning occurs. If the information on which needs were established is inaccurate, if wrong interpretations were made, or if incorrect conclusions were drawn regarding its meaning, position numbers and qualifications will be unreliable. Unreliable data can involve costly errors in over- and under-planning. Dollars can be wasted, company goals may be unmet, and human disruptions can occur.

The impact of establishing numbers and qualifications deserves the support, personal attention, and involvement of all levels of management. Every supervisor should be concerned that his or her planning make provision for having available the human contribution when needed. Every individual employee should be concerned that he or she is needed in the position when and where assigned and that it will make maximum use of his or her time and talents. Appropriate establishment of human needs makes provision for the company to plan for human requirements and for the individual to make the expected contribution. This can assure the maximum ROI in human resources, whereas inaccurate determination of needs will result in human resource waste and a low ROI.

7

Inventorying, matching, and acquiring human resources

After determining human resource needs—the numbers, the qualifications, and the dates—then what? Some needs must be met immediately. For example, the assistant treasurer's position is open and should have been filled a month ago. Who in our human resource inventory qualifies? If no one, how should we proceed to fill the position from the outside?

The new wing of the Northside Plant is scheduled to begin operations October 1 of next year. The organization chart has been completed. The number of additional people has been determined and the required positions and skills ascertained. The next decision is where these people will be obtained. Who can be transferred or promoted from within the company? What about replacements for these people? Since there is some lead time, how many and which individuals can be trained for these positions? For positions that must be filled from the outside, when and how will the recruiting be handled?

The key factors in inventorying are numbers, competency, skills, trainability, and potential. Also, a determination should be made concerning the future availability of the inventory as in-

fluenced by separations, retirements, and policies or practices re-
stricting mobility. It should be assumed that if the company has an
appropriate training and development program, many of the individuals needed will become qualified and thus will be promoted to
fill anticipated openings.

INVENTORYING AVAILABLE RESOURCES

What resources are now available? What will be the degree of
dependability of this resource over the period of time covered by
the plan? An inventory should cover these items:

Total number of people available.

Present number of people in each type of position or job classification.

Skills and qualifications available but not presently being used
—for example, the accountant who is a production supervisor.

Age distribution of total group and for each job category—how
many will be retiring and when?

Predictable losses: planned retirements, discharges, resignations, early retirements, health problems, failures to qualify
for scheduled promotions, deaths. Past history, trends, actuarial tables, and similar data will shed considerable light on
these numbers.

The form shown in Figure 2 enables managers and human
resource planners to anticipate losses on the basis of specific job
titles and dates. It forces recognition that the available human resource inventory is not static, but that it is experiencing constantly
occurring loss that must be accurately anticipated. This inventory
provides one of the crucial ingredients in the human resource
planning process.

Naturally an inventory will include employee's backgrounds,
qualifications, availability, career aspirations, current promotability
and future potential. It will also take into consideration the legal
aspects of the utilization of available human resources—compliance with all requirements regarding training, promotions, discharges, pay, and age.

Figure 2. Projection of manpower losses.

Date _____

Location or Division _____

Estimate turnover based on voluntary and involuntary terminations. Include retirements, anticipated separations due to illness, and other losses that can be
projected on the basis of past trends.

JOB TITLE	1975	1976	1977	1978	1979	1980
Manager	___	___	___	___	___	___
Assistant Manager	___	___	___	___	___	___
Production Manager	___	___	___	___	___	___
Operations Manager	___	___	___	___	___	___
Sales Manager	___	___	___	___	___	___
Personnel Manager	___	___	___	___	___	___
Advertising Manager	___	___	___	___	___	___
Display Manager	___	___	___	___	___	___
Security Manager	___	___	___	___	___	___
Division Managers	___	___	___	___	___	___
Others	___	___	___	___	___	___

The human resource inventory should be sufficiently comprehensive, systematically organized and stored, and readily retriev-
able to enable management to make the most prudent decisions
regarding utilization and promotions. The purpose of a complete
and constantly updated inventory is to:

—Make available to management the information needed in
making decisions about people.
—Identify deficiencies and opportunities for improvement in
skills, education, or experience that could be enhanced
through training, job restructuring, or job reassignment.
—Measure how well talents and qualifications are being utilized
on present jobs to determine whether transfers may be in
order.
—Project the potential of individuals.
—Identify the overall and specific individual strengths and
weaknesses in various areas of the company.
—Identify gaps when comparing company needs with available

Figure 3. Form for recording data on all middle and upper management in a specific location.

DATE _____

EMPLOYEE NAME	AGE	EMPL. DATE	POSITION (also enter merchandise areas if applicable)	$ SALES VALUE	TOTAL SALARY LAST YEAR	CURRENT DRAW	*TRAINING PROGRAMS ATTENDED	**PROMOTION AVAILABILITY STATUS

*Please use abbreviations indicated:

Junior Executive Development — JED
In-Store — IS   Shoe School — SS
American Management Associations — AMA
Professional Development — PDP

Advertising School — AS
Management Development — MDP
Home Fashions School — HFS
Display School — DS

**Please use probability codes
1. Ready for promotion
2. Promotable within one to two years
3. Limited to present position
4. Present performance unsatisfactory

inventory—gaps that will need to be filled through development, promotions, or employment from the outside.

Figure 3 provides a profile of the qualifications, availability, and promotability of key management personnel. It is designed to bring together a variety of pertinent information necessary in the evaluation of the key human resources of a company or operating unit to correct identified surpluses or gaps.

An inventory identifies how well the individual is measuring up to the requirements of the present job, what he or she might be capable of doing, and the nature of what must be done to qualify him or her to reach the next level in the organization. This not only assures the maximum utilization and growth for all human resources but also becomes the propelling force that moves the company forward. The availability of capable human resources enables the company to be constantly responsive to its changing environment, both within and without.

The first priority is current jobs filled and performances that ensure an efficient, profitable operation. The second priority is concern for what happens in the future—filling subsequent job openings with qualified individuals.

ANALYSIS OF THE INVENTORY

A comprehensive inventory also reveals certain things about the past history and current status of human resource utilization. Often, individuals are identified who have dead-ended, suffered career arrest, or are stymied. Once identified, steps should be taken to determine reasons. It might be the fault of the individual—having refused a transfer or promotion. Possibly a selfish manager has attempted unfairly to hide or retain the individual in his or her own department. In other instances the company's system, or operation of that system, has failed to provide for the employee's career progress. The stagnant career should be analyzed, as would any other static company resource. Can it be improved, enlarged, or changed to make a greater contribution? Not all employees who are dropouts from career progression can be reactivated or salvaged. However, both the company and the individual deserve the opportunity to try to protect the investment each has already made.

Just as the company makes every effort to use its machinery and financial resources for maximum return, the same effort should be the guiding principle regarding human resources. This is not done solely for the benefit of the company but also as a means of providing additional career opportunity, compensation, and security for the individual. In other words, both the organization and the individual benefit.

The system used for recording, storing, and retrieving the human resource inventory can range from index cards to computer programs. Generally, smaller companies trend to simpler systems because they are adequate for their needs. More sophisticated programs must be used where thousands of employees and/or hundreds of domestic and foreign locations are involved. However, even smaller companies should have adequate systems in order to be competitive with larger companies regarding the proper inventorying of human resources.

GAUGING COMPETENCY AND PERFORMANCE

While conducting a Presidents Roundtable for the Presidents Association of the American Management Associations, I asked a group of presidents their most difficult task. The answer was "evaluation of job performance," with particular reference to knowing how to interpret or rate the rater. This chore represents frustration for most managers, even though precisely drawn objectives and standards and the use of all elements of professional management provide an objective measurement of criteria.

It should be recognized that some form of evaluation of competency and performance occurs regardless of the sophistication level of the system. Historically, this judgment consisted of a personal opinion regarding pay increases, transfers, promotions, discharges, and other decisions based on people value. Judgments were generally made only when decisions were needed. This subjective judgment became part of the value placed on available human resource inventory.

The fairness and value of this type of informal judgment is almost totally inadequate in meeting today's demands for more accurate utilization of human resources and in meeting government regulations regarding people decisions. Regardless of the exact system being used for evaluating current competency and performance, care should be taken to ensure that individuals doing the evaluation understand the system. Instructions should be given on completion of the rating forms and on conducting follow-up interviews. Next, the system should be tested on various individuals and levels of employees so that they are informed regarding its operation and that their support is elicited. Finally, results must be constantly analyzed to determine whether the factors being rated are pertinent to actual performance success.

The more complete and accurate the performance expectation, and the more quantified the measuring instruments, the more reliable the rating will be. Also, if the rater and the person being rated can agree on numerically established expectations ahead of time, both are in a better position to judge whether goals and standards have been met. This increases the rater's self-confidence in gauging performance and the individual's acceptance of the rating.

The significance attached to gauging competency and performance is a direct reflection of the company's basic philosophy and people-related systems. If the company-implemented system shows that compensation and/or promotional opportunities are relatively unaffected by quantity and quality of individual contribution, then performance evaluation has limited relevance. However, if the competency and contribution by the individual become the basis for compensation, future development, and individual career charting and promotions, an adequate system—fully implemented—becomes essential. The evaluation can be the key link in the whole system of human resource planning and utilization.

These are specific goals for measuring competency and performance as they relate to inventorying human resources:

To determine the individual and collective performance of the human resource.

To identify promotable individuals on the basis of performance.

To identify deficiencies and opportunities for improvement in order to improve current performance.

To identify and forecast future potential.

To identify individual development and training needs.

To analyze the availability of human resources—on the basis of competency, performance, and potential—for meeting the current and future needs of the company.

This list does not contain all the purposes and goals of a job performance evaluation program but primarily those that relate to the inventorying of human resources. The individual's right to know where he or she stands, and the evaluation as a basis for compensation, are the types of goals not included in the list.

GUIDES FOR APPRAISING JOB PERFORMANCE

Evaluation involves judging employees on the basis of their overall performance, contribution, and relationship to the company. The system should be fair and accurate from the viewpoint of both the company and the individual. There must be an initial and continuing effort to construct and maintain the best system possible on an objective and measurable basis. The evaluation should be viewed as both a link in the company's efforts to meet its future needs and a guide to the individual's entitlement to merit consideration.

The whole system of human resource planning becomes questionable unless the evaluation systems provide reliable information that can be creditably used as a basis for decision making. Although essential during normal times, they become vital to the survival of the company and to the lives of countless employees in times of rapid growth or various changes within the company.

One approach to evaluation of the competencies and skills of human resources is the technique of employee analysis. This is concerned with how well a specific employee is carrying out the tasks that constitute his or her job. It identifies the behavior change required to improve the employee's job performance and information that should serve as the basis for his or her training and development. Employee analysis involves such quantitative criteria as number of units produced in a given period of time, quality of units produced, cost of material used for producing each unit, cost of machinery and its maintenance, and various other indications of how well the employee is producing as compared with others in similar positions. For sales or management jobs, the criteria for analysis would be different, but the principles of measurement would be similar.

The appraisal of individual performance has been around for a long time, but the search for more reliable and precise measurement has led to the development of special appraisal forms and programs for various positions throughout the company. The forms should be kept simple but should be geared to the job concerned. Evaluation should be regarded as a positive tool for guiding and encouraging better performance and growth. Accurate, fair judgments of others and their performance are difficult, but they can be made more reliably if the supervisors involved are thoroughly instructed regarding the skills and techniques required.

The evaluation form shown in Figure 4 provides a formal system for evaluating job performance as a basis for decisions regarding compensation, promotability, and analysis of human resources.

Appraisals should give a reliable picture of the individual at work, rate the performance against some standard or expectation, and serve as the basis for dialog between the immediate supervisor and the employee regarding job performance and how improvements can be made for the benefit of the employee and the company. Management can use the information as a tool for understanding the strengths and weaknesses of the individual as they relate to job performance, for deciding on salary increases, transfers, promotions, reassignments, and terminations, and for helping the employee in making the most of his or her abilities and attaining a sense of satisfaction through the performance of the job.

Various details and forms used for the many aspects of job performance evaluation will not be considered in depth at this point since they have been covered in two previous books.[1] Also, numerous management experts and psychological leaders have researched and reported at length regarding the various systems and techniques for appraisal of job performance. Regardless of the system, simple or complex, it should be sufficient to provide management with an accurate summation of the current performance level of the individual. Knowledge of individual and collective competency constitutes a key consideration regarding the value placed on current human resources. This also becomes the development and planning base for future utilization.

[1] Ray A. Killian, *Managers Must Lead!* and *The Working Woman,* AMACOM, 1966 and 1971.

Figure 4. A typical job evaluation form.

Employee's Name _____ Date _____

Job Title_____ Department _____

INSTRUCTIONS: Complete the following review on exempt employees without major supervisory responsibility prior to determining a salary increase recommendation.

Each factor should be assigned a point value from 1 to 5 as follows:
   1 = Unsatisfactory; 2 = Below Standard; 3 = Satisfactory; 4 = Above Standard; 5 = Outstanding, consistently well above standard.

Use the "Comments" section following each statement to explain why the assigned rating was given, being as specific as possible. Refer to special documentation of performance in file and compare performance with agreed-upon goals. EACH SECTION MUST HAVE COMMENTS INCLUDED. Increases will not be processed unless all portions of the form are completed.

Point Value

1. DECISION MAKING
Makes sound, logical, and timely decisions without undue supervisory guidance.
Comments: _____ _____

2. CREATIVENESS AND INITIATIVE
Shows imagination and originality in work. Not afraid of trying new approaches and ideas.
Comments: _____ _____

3. PLANNING
Anticipates future problems and situations. Plans to provide for efficient day-to-day operations, while providing contingencies for the unexpected.
Comments:_____ _____

4. COST CONTROL
Ability to maximize utilization of available funds and stay within budget constraints.
Comments: _____ _____

5. SERVICE ATTITUDE
Works closely with management to give professional opinions and guidance on improving overall profitability. Does so while maintaining good rapport with all areas (services, stores, and public).
Comments:_____ _____

Point
Value

6. **TECHNICAL COMPETENCE**   Has good working knowledge in the technical areas of involvement. Antici- pates problems and provides inputs for effectively dealing with them. Gives staff assistance to department or others as needed.
Comments: _____   _____

7. **ABILITY TO COMMUNICATE AND IMPLE- MENT IDEAS**   Writes clear, concise reports and/or verbalizes ideas clearly and effec- tively. Assists in the implementation of programs related to the area of technical competence.
Comments: _____   _____

8. **QUALITY OF WORK**   Work is accurate with only normal number of mistakes.
Comments: _____   _____

9. **QUANTITY OF WORK**   Produces satisfactory volume of work for the area of involvement.
Comments: _____   _____

10. **TOTAL JOB PERFORMANCE**   Consider all aspects of the job that are not covered by the other categories, such as presenting timely reports, giving sufficient attention to reports to ensure that full knowledge is being utilized, etc. Other intangibles, such as attitude, co- operation, loyalty, job interest, etc., should be considered.
Comments: _____   _____

TOTAL RATING (Total of Items 1 through 10)   _____

_____

Signature of Rater _____

The following are the types of information generally essential for a comprehensive evaluation.

—Results of performance as measured against expectations and standards.

—In the case of management personnel: quality of leadership as indicated by decision-making ability, development of others, delegation, creativity, intelligence, communications skills, expertise in job performance, knowledge of all aspects of the job, employee relations skills, results produced by those supervised, attitude, planning and various administrative skills, tough-mindedness, and overall quality of supervision.

—In the case of nonsupervisory personnel: quantity and quality of work results, cooperation and dependability, job interest, attitude, interest in growth, and motivational level as it might relate to current results or as a basis for improvement.

—Change, if any, since the last evaluation. Is there evidence of improvement or decline in performance?

—Identification of areas of greatest strength and opportunities for change or improvement.

—Whether the individual is in need of improvement, is adequate where he or she is, or is ready for promotion.

Evaluation is often an unpopular activity in the minds of those being evaluated. Unfortunately, it involves judgment of people and, too often, nonquantitative opinions of how well they are performing on the job. The increased education and the changing lifestyles of the typical employee minimize the right of anyone to sit in judgment of others. However, the fact remains that decisions have to be made regarding compensation, job security, training, and promotions. Often this involves choosing one individual out of a group. Although, admittedly, evaluations lack scientific preciseness, they remain the best means available for making people-related decisions.

The importance of the task and its far-reaching impact impose a heavy responsibility on those involved in providing and implementing evaluation systems. The following checkpoints should be useful.

1. A test of the reliability of goals set and the extent to which these have been communicated and understood.

2. The physical environment: efficiency of tools, machines, and other pertinent details that determine the individual's opportunity to produce results.
3. Research and validation of the instrument or form used for evaluation purposes.
4. Thorough training and genuine interest on the part of those engaged in doing the evaluation.
5. Comprehensive communications to those who are to be rated regarding the purpose and method of the rating.
6. A constructive interview with every individual, oriented toward future opportunity for growth, not criticism of past activities.
7. Appropriate confidentiality and use of results for beneficial decision making.

The instrument has to be designed to provide the required information. This information must then be properly used in the overall human resource planning system.

PREDICTING POTENTIAL AND PROMOTABILITY

For every company and individual, the future is more important than the past. Nothing can be done about the time and resources already a part of history. Managing, planning, decision making, and human resource planning are primarily future-oriented. The inventory of human resources is for the purpose of determining what is available for future use, development, and filling of needs. What a company becomes in the future depends almost entirely on its people and the decisions made by and about them today.

A part of most evaluation programs is the judgment or "guesstimate" of what the future potential and promotability will be. This involves answers to the questions:

Is the individual promotable now and, if so, to what position? If not promotable now, when?
What improvement or change must occur before he or she will be ready for promotion?
How far up the ladder is the individual likely to climb—one

more rung, or is there potential for going all the way to the top?

To what extent can this individual be counted on to meet the company's future need to change, grow, and expand its purpose in business?

The judgment regarding potential and promotability is made in relationship to what the company will probably be like in the future. The focus is first on determining future company needs and then on the potential of the individual as he or she might be expected to fit into those future plans. Each side of the equation must be known before gaps can be identified and a match-up achieved.

The whole system of meeting future needs depends on success in identifying and predicting accurately which individuals can be expected to move up and what must be done to make certain that they are qualified when needed. Companies have developed an almost endless variety of tests, games, gimmicks, and programs for spotting and evaluating managerial ability, often even before the individual has been given managerial responsibility, including job assignment tests designed to determine how well the individual performs in a given situation, psychological tests, and individual or group evaluation of ability and potential.

There are assessment centers that generally combine tests, games, simulation, individual and group interviews, overall assessment of experience and performance as they might relate to future potential, and finally group judgment by company operating executives. The American Management Associations has developed a complete program of materials and training for the implementation of an assessment center. Generally, an executive in the company is assigned responsibility for running the program and is trained in the techniques of assessment along with several other operating managers. Companies that make extensive use of this technique might not consider an individual promotable beyond certain levels until he or she receives a favorable rating by the assessment center.

By far the most universally used is the technique of projecting past experience into the future—assuming that the batting average today represents the type of expectations likely in the future. In a company this process is basically the same as in the military—

moving up the ladder a rung at a time and being relatively uncon-
cerned whether the first-line supervisor in the XYZ Sheet Metal
Company has the potential for top management or whether the
second lieutenant can ever be expected to become a general.

These approaches still leave most companies frustrated and
with a less than glowing statistical record of success in the accuracy
of early identification of managerial potential. This does not minimize the importance of the need to make every effort to spot and
develop as fully as possible those individuals who will be leading
the company in the future.

The difficulty lies in the lack of valid types of models for
management success. Some successful managers have professional
educations—law, accounting, education, engineering, or business.
Some have limited educations (although relatively few today).
Managerial traits—mental, physical, and emotional—vary widely.
Yet just as the college recruiter looks at a high school athlete and
judges his fundamental, innate potential, so must management
make decisions regarding the potential of its human resources.

RELATING POTENTIAL TO JOB GOALS

Regardless of the system or technique used, the goal is to look
at job requirements and to predict the type of executive characteristics and performance that will produce desired results. This
leads to an identification of managerial traits most likely to result
in executive success. These often include intelligence, integrity,
durability, sensitivity, decisiveness, courage, will to win, ability to
work through others, flexibility, salesmanship skills, skills in planning, organizing, and communications, teaching ability, and motivation. Lists vary, and every management expert—whether inside
or outside the company—has his or her own list of favorites and
order of priority. These requirements are often separated into
categories such as skills, mental abilities, aptitudes, interests, and
motivational characteristics.

Once the list has been identified and jobs adequately defined
or described, the next step is to determine which qualifications are
possessed by each managerial candidate. It is for this purpose that
tests, management games, simulation, and subjective judgment are
used. Wilbert E. Scheer, in appraising future potential, wrote:

In summary, it can be said that Appraisal of Potential is actually a rating of probable future performance in the same or the next job. It considers such factors as:

1. *Goal setting and attainment*—the direction of the work and the scheduling to remain on target.

2. *Results*—a record of exceeding overall standards in terms of quantity, quality, improvements, costs, employee relations, and responsibilities.

3. *Pressure*—performance during times and periods of stress.

4. *Knowledge of the business*—understanding of policies and programs beyond own area of specialization.

5. *Decision making*—willingness to "stick . . . neck out" by giving prompt and decisive answers, and . . . batting average based on decisions that turned out to be appropriate, effective, timely, and acceptable.

6. *Originality and resourcefulness*—ability to come up through the hard crust of accustomed ideas with a fresh approach.

7. *Outstanding achievements*—leadership experiences in and out of the business that have proved their worth.

8. *Judgment*—the knack of distinguishing between what is pertinent and what is irrelevant in relation to work, time, and ideas.

9. *Independence*—the fine balance between being able to act for himself and still operate within corporate policy, fiscal policy, operational, contractual, and legal constraints.

10. *Relationships*—awareness of the effects of his actions on others at all levels, whose feelings, authoritative opinions, and judgments must be respected.[2]

It can be assumed that most individuals want a better job and want to make more money. They should be interested in finding ways to achieve aspirations with their present company and should be willing to respond to reasonable efforts to move them toward the achievement of those desires. If the company expects to move forward, it must make plans for a different future, and so must the individual. Progressive companies generally take the initiative in making better jobs available, as well as in providing opportunities for individuals to prepare themselves for those jobs.

The company's human resource utilization should provide the system whereby the most qualified individuals are moved into the

[2] Wilbert E. Scheer, *Corporate Growth Through Internal Management Development* (Chicago, Ill., 1952), The Dartnell Corporation, p. 120.

better jobs. It should be apparent that the company cannot be competitive with obsolete plans or systems. Company self-interest requires programs for identifying and appraising the future potential of people just as effectively as it forecasts production and marketing opportunities.

The company must be constantly open-minded and alert for better methods for identifying and appraising people potential. Methods currently available for doing this are neither precise nor infallible. Identifying potential deserves management's time and resources to develop and implement systems that will ensure the availability of the best possible job candidates. This activity is generally initiated and refined through the use of internal specialists, obtaining and adapting programs from the outside (AMA's Assessment Center Program, tests, and so on) and comparing programs with other companies.

Most companies have discovered that excessive recruitment of experienced employees from the outside is unreliable as well as expensive. Often, executive success in one type of company environment fails to guarantee similar success in a different climate. The conclusion by companies is to develop most of their own future human resource needs.

MATCHING NEEDS AND RESOURCES: THE SUCCESSION PLAN

The match-up begins with an awareness of needs—specific positions, qualifications for each, and times when positions should be filled. The next step is a look at the inventory available—numbers, qualifications, probable development, predictable losses, promotability profiles, and forecast of potential. The matching involves fitting pieces of the puzzle into place, one at a time. It also includes actuarial statistics and company experience related to deaths, separations, promotional failure, development and training success, and other types of input where predictions regarding individuals might not be reliable while statistical norms for the whole group would be.

An example of matching might involve the retirement of the supply department supervisor at the end of next year and a search for a replacement. Who is qualified? Who could be promoted?

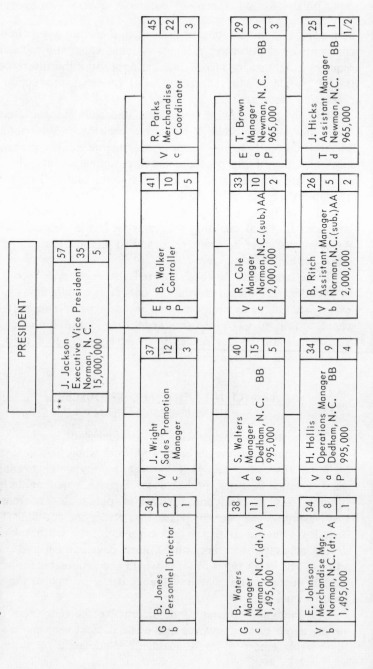

Figure 5. Organization chart showing profile of structure, relationship of positions, inventory of incumbents, and possible need for replacement.

1. Name	6. Age
2. Title	7. Length of Service
3. Store Name and Classification	8. Time in Job
4. Volume	
5. Performance and Potential Codes	

1. Name — First name/middle initial/last name.
2. Title — Example: Mgr., Branch Mgr., Asst. Mgr., Mdse. Mgr., or Opns. Mgr.
3. Store Name and Classification.
4. Total sales volume.
5. Performance and Potential Codes (see below).
6. Age in years.
7. Length of service — number of years of unbroken service with company.
8. Time in job — number of years in current position.

PERFORMANCE CODE

E – Excellent   — Represents the top 10% of all executives in all categories.

V – Very Good   — Represents upper 25% in performance and generally indicates a high level of achievement of objectives.

G – Good   — Represents the level of performance expected from most of our experienced executives and indicates upper-middle levels of performance.

A – Adequate   — Represents the minimum level of performance that is acceptable under usual circumstances.

U – Unsatisfactory   — Represents an unsatisfactory level of performance and indicates that failure to improve will result in termination or change of position.

T – Too New to Rate

POTENTIAL CODE

a. Promotable now. One of two sub-designations must be made:

     P — "up" — will indicate readiness for promotion to a higher level.

     L — "lateral" — will indicate readiness for lateral promotion or transfer.

b. Promotable within 2 years or less.

c. Potentially promotable — time uncertain.

d. Potential good, but at present level only.

e. Potential and future is questionable.

Who is the most logical choice when all influences are considered? How soon should the individual be moved into the job?

Matching might also involve thousands of employees and the use of computers. A major midwestern oil company considered the age of its president and, according to the company retirement policy, knew that he would have to be replaced on a certain date. The criteria or minimum qualifications were put into the computer, along with the qualifications of potential candidates in the company. A person several levels below top management was identified and groomed and proved to be a very successful president.

The form shown in Figure 5 is used by a major department store group. Note that the purpose is to determine the current performance and contribution level, time and type of promotability at present, and potential in the future. Potential replacements are also identified for various positions. This becomes a top-level profile of management human resources for each unit that can then be cross-matched with similar reports from all other units. The president of the company states that this information is extremely important to the company and that it is reviewed regularly.

It is not my intention to imply or recommend that people should be shifted like chessmen, according to the whims of the player, without adequate consideration for individual interests and preferences. A major thrust of ROI human resource planning should take into consideration employees' wishes. Although the company cannot cater to all personal preferences, an effort should be made to balance the needs of the company with those of the individual so that the mutual interests of both will be served.

The nature of the human resource inventory will be significantly affected by the individual's willingness to accept transfers, promotions, job changes, and new situations. Individual planning is one means of discovering the career interests of each employee. Too often the company makes plans regarding people without consideration for their willingness to comply or for the impact of the action on their lives. The awareness of the needs and preferences of individuals will be a major consideration in future human resource planning. From this data, human resource charts, succession flow, and movement forecasts can be developed in a more considerate, realistic manner.

Matching involves long-range planning, operational plans, and plans for meeting unexpected and emergency situations. Appropriate long-range human resource planning, which should include certain contingency life preservers, can avoid most of the panic decisions. Unplanned replacements and promotions often involve failures and regrets. Also, temporary assignments or "acting managers" are seldom as satisfactory as having the right permanent placements available when needed. This does not negate the necessity to make an emergency replacement at times to keep the shop running or a sales manager in the territory.

The need for accurate, quick match-up is the main reason large companies store this type of information in computers, where it is accurate and quickly available. Management can make better decisions regarding people if it has all the information needed at crucial times. Computers can be of inestimable value in matching needs and resources.

IDENTIFYING CURRENT AND FUTURE GAPS

The first responsibility of human resource planning is filling existing openings. The plan should become operative to fill every possible position through transfers and promotions from within. Whenever a position remains unfilled and expectations are not met, a failure has occurred in the human resource plan. If no one is available for promotion to the manager's position at plant Y and production begins slipping, human resource planning has failed to meet its goal.

Potential successors should be identified in advance to ensure that positions will be filled on a timely basis by a qualified replacement. The form shown in Figure 6 will help in identifying possible replacements.

Amount of lead time deserves special attention in determining whether candidates will be available when needed. Lead-time considerations and action to minimize gaps might include:

Delaying, where practical, the occurrence of a vacancy. Possibly retirement can be delayed until a replacement is ready.
Delaying the transfer or promotion, provided that it can be done with minimum damage to the career of the individual or to the available position.

Figure 6. Form showing company succession plan.

POSITION	HELD BY	AGE	POTENTIAL SUCCESSORS	RATINGS					
				A	B	C	D	E	F

RATING OF SUCCESSORS AS TO
THEIR MAJOR SKILLS

A: _____   D: _____
B: _____   E: _____
C: _____   F: _____

Source: Lloyd J. Hughlett, "Long-Range Planning Implemented by Management by Objectives" (Boone, N.C.: Executive Resources Development Institute, Inc.).

Speeding up the training and development process in order to qualify the replacement quicker.

Considering cross-transferring or promotions from other skill or discipline areas.

Providing for limited surpluses for unpredictable emergencies.

How much lead time is really necessary to qualify an assistant to replace a branch bank manager? The company should have general guideline answers from similar situations and a specific answer in this instance. Too much lead time can cause frustrations on the part of individuals and wasted human resources on the part of the company. It is highly desirable for all concerned that the lead time be as precise as possible.

Emergencies generally occur when shrinkage of potential replacements has not been accurately calculated or when the human resource fails to provide maximum flexibility. Most companies have statistics available, based on their own experience and from other sources, regarding the number of deaths that will occur at various age levels, the number and levels of separations of people from company employment (these could be either employee- or employer-initiated), the number of temporary or permanent disabilities likely to occur, the number of individuals unpromotable currently or at various levels in the future, and the number of failures to properly assess future changes in the company that affect position needs and times at which needed.

Company plotting might be compared to my experience as a carrier-based fighter pilot in the navy. It was necessary to do our own navigation. A great aid was a template on which land masses and identifiable points were outlined on clear plastic. The template was inserted into the plotting board and the position, direction, and speed of the carrier noted. It was then possible to anticipate where the carrier would be at the expected landing time and the flight pattern to and from targets. Minute-to-minute plotting, changes in course, plane speed, wind, and so on, were constantly being reflected or updated, but we always knew the current position in relation to land masses and the fleet. Human resource gaps should constantly reflect what the company needs, the present position relative to available or developable resources, and the gap between the two.

PLANS FOR ACQUIRING HUMAN RESOURCES

Any activity that is not mathematically precise is subject to inaccuracies, overlaps, and gaps. This is another way of saying that, even with the best human resource planning, some openings will occur that must be filled through outside recruiting. However, many major companies promote so universally from within that the only higher-level people recruited outside the ranks are professionals, such as lawyers, and then only at the entry level for that position. Many companies, on the other hand, don't care or they permit faulty planning to create gaps that cannot be filled through regular channels. The real question is where to find needed people. Many will, according to plan, come from lower-level management positions, and some candidates in lower ranks will get a second look if the situation becomes critical. Many can be recruited into junior executive positions and groomed for promotion. Increasingly, women and minority groups will be considered. And, finally, some might have to be recruited from other firms.

The initial step in filling every position should be to search internally. Where electronic data processing is available, the search is generally for all candidates who are qualified and for whom the positions to be filled would represent a promotion or advantageous lateral move. The principles are basically the same even when less formal searches are used. Regardless of the system used, there should be an understanding that no decisions will be made or any communication attempted with any internal candidate until there is clearance through an established control point—one that has minimal vested interest in the outcome. This can avoid short-circuiting the system by would-be kingmakers or by promoting personal favorites.

Full consideration should also be given to candidates produced by training and development. It is reasonable to assume that individuals are learning and gaining experience on the job and that development programs should be contributing to the production of qualified candidates for most positions above entry level. Advance planning will identify potential promotables, and the specific grooming of these individuals can ensure their being qualified when positions become available.

One company goes a step beyond posting openings internally

by including in all recruitment ads the statement, "All present employees are invited to apply for the job being advertised if they are interested and feel they are qualified."

Depending on the nature of the position to be filled and the urgency of filling it, a variety of recruitment steps, techniques, and sources should be used. These might include:

1. A review of applications in the file.

2. Present employees (especially those in positions similar to the opening) might be asked to make referrals.

3. Various forms of advertising—classified, professional journals, and college alumni publications.

4. Contacts with professional organizations of individuals of the type being sought. Many of these organizations maintain registers and placement services.

5. A placement agency that will seek out and make referrals of qualified individuals listed with them. Either the individual or the company pays the agency fee, or it may be split or negotiated. Many agencies will make referrals only to companies that agree to pay the fee. This usually amounts to about 20 percent of the annual starting salary. Of course, government agencies such as the Employment Security Commission make no charge for referrals.

6. A search firm that will embark on a search to locate and refer qualified candidates. In most instances, the search firm will charge a set fee or a percentage of the salary stated for the job as a fee. Typically, the fee must be paid regardless of whether referrals result in filling the position.

Recruiting from the outside is expensive and is often a last-resort approach to filling a position. The costs for filling a $20,000 salary position is shown in Table 1. Over and above this expense, there remains the uncertainty of whether the person will like the company and whether his or her family will find the new location acceptable. There are many instances in which the employee or family became unhappy and return to their original location. Regardless of how well qualified, the new outsider might require six months to a year on the job before becoming fully oriented into the peculiarities of the new company. Another consideration is the effect on morale of lower-level employees when they learned that a better position has been filled from the outside. It is true that some of these expenses and uncertainties might exist if a

Table 1. Cost to fill a $20,000 salary position.

Various forms of advertising	$ 400
Travel for interviews	750
Executive interview time	600
Agency fee	4,000
Travel and other expenses for employee and family to check housing	800
Moving expenses and other related costs	2,000
Real estate fees (if paid)	5,000
Total	$13,550

promotion were made from within, but it seldom involves as much expense or uncertainty as bringing in a stranger from the outside.

The most common error that forces management to direct its recruitment efforts to the outside is inaccurate assessment of its own candidates. A president, in reviewing the personnel jackets on five candidates for a top divisional position, concluded that all of them seemed to have certain faults or weaknesses that, in his opinion, barred them from consideration. The company eventually employed an experienced person from a competitor. It developed that he had far more shortcomings than any of the company candidates. Thousands of dollars' worth of lost business later, the man was separated through mutual agreement. One of the five original candidates, although not ideally qualified, was promoted and performed admirably in the position.

The weaknesses of the internal candidate are often overexposed, while those of the outsider are underexposed. This can result in lesser-qualified individuals being employed at greater expense and risk to the company. Factors like this provide the most convincing argument for comprehensive human resource planning that will enable the company to meet most of its needs from within.

KEEPING THE HUMAN RESOURCE
INVENTORY UPDATED

Can company needs be met at present? Can these needs be met successfully in the future? Does our inventory provide an ongoing program of information regarding the number, performance levels, and qualifications of everyone on the payroll? Do we feel comfortable about the validity of our forecasts concerning future potential and promotability? Are our plans adequate for successfully filling all positions on schedule with highly qualified individuals either from internal sources or from outside? If we can answer these questions affirmatively, our attention can then be directed to training and development—the method for improving competency and raising qualifications for increased company contribution.

8
Developing full performance and potential

When being urged to implement a company training program, a New York executive responded, "The only training I believe in is 'monkey see, monkey do.' " A Dallas bank president, in reviewing the budget requests for the coming year, observed, "I sometimes get the feeling that we're in the education business instead of running a bank. We seem to devote more time, attention, and money to training than to managing our money and operating the bank." Perhaps somewhere between these two positions the right answer can be found regarding the proper role of training and development in managing human resources.

The overall function of training has been defined as "the process of aiding employees to gain effectiveness in their present and future work." The company purchases raw material and, through processing, achieves an added value, which can be sold at a profit. Human time and potential are purchased as raw material that can be converted through the processing of training and leadership influence into value-added profit. The potential for added value, through human growth and development, represents the greatest tappable resource already available. This potential can be realized through the development of appropriate habits of thought and action, skills, knowledge, and attitude. In this sense, companies never really have to make a choice of whether to train, but rather what type of training.

Training can be the trial-and-error, hit-or-miss, learn-by-experience, costly-mistake variety, or the training experiences can be deliberately and conceptually designed to bring about desirable job behavior and results in the quickest, most economical manner. It is difficult to find accurate answers to the following questions in carrying out training functions.

—How does the improvement of performance and future potential of people on the payroll contribute to the overall human resource planning program?

—Does training really pay off—is there a return on investment?

—Should training and development be left to outside agencies?

—How much time, personnel, and budget should be devoted to training?

—What types of training are most effective?

—Can we really justify taking people off production lines and out of sales offices to sit in a classroom?

—How can we get our executives and personnel really interested in the importance of training?

—Is training worthwhile if people don't want it? Can it be forced?

—How can we make decisions regarding the types of training needed and the ways in which it will be conducted?

—Where and how can we really find the answers to the expensive questions regarding the many canned training programs and visual aids?

—Can we adequately measure and justify the results of training? How?

TRAINING ASSUMPTIONS

Many major business decisions are aided by making certain assumptions and examining the various alternatives available. This procedure seems applicable in approaching the training issue. Prudent companies often follow this line of reasoning.

—The company is unable to employ people at acceptable pay

levels from the outside who can perform satisfactorily without some additional training.

—If the company is to increase production and sales, improve quality, give better customer service, and maintain competitive leadership, all employees must make a greater contribution than they are currently making.

—If the company expects to change and grow, it will require additional amounts and types of leadership at all levels.

—If the company assumes and plans for various types of shrinkage of human resources at all levels—resignations, terminations, retirements, job failures, and the like—it must be responsible for its replacement.

—If training is to be justified, it must tie directly into and make a measurable contribution to company key result areas—production, sales, and profits.

Human resource planning requires facing up to these facts and finding the most logical answers. The company must correctly assume that new employees are to be given training and that employees already on the payroll must improve if the company is to grow and remain competitive. This essential ingredient for improvement must be provided on a systematic, results-oriented basis.

IDENTIFYING DEVELOPMENT GOALS

Progressive companies assume a responsibility for meeting the two key goals of training and development, namely, improvement of performance in the current job and preparation for increased job responsibility. The overall goals of development should be:

1. Concern for the future of the business—its maximum goal achievement.

2. Identifying and defining specific job behavior and performance changes needed.

3. Providing for the maximum utilization of the present and future potential of all human resources.

4. Ensuring that human development planning and other areas of company planning are integrated so that each will be complementary and make its expected contribution.

5. Providing for the career growth of individuals and ensuring their retention and motivated contribution.

6. Planning for the availability of qualified replacements when needed.

7. Enabling the company to grow by ensuring that vital human resources will be available to meet the specific position qualifications needed.

8. Providing programs and systems whereby individuals will reach acceptable productivity levels quicker and more economically.

9. Providing growth whereby individuals will qualify for greater responsibility quickly and with more certainty of success.

10. Improving efficiency and effectiveness in every job.

11. Maintaining and improving all outside relationships through the delivery of all products and services on time and in good order.

Not all qualifications and people problems can be solved through training. Training cannot provide solutions to an ineffective human organization or antiquated physical facilities. It is not a substitute for inadequate compensation or benefits. It will not fill the vacuum created by negative or improper leadership. Management's major responsibility should be to identify the valid role training and development can be expected to make and then ensure that this is achieved.

VALID EXPECTATIONS FROM THE DEVELOPMENT FUNCTION

The greatest immediate and most visible impact should be on individual and overall job results. You will know that training and development are succeeding when there is a change in the individual's job behavior or performance—that is, when unwanted behavior is being reduced and there is evidence of acceptable new responses. You will see improvement in the individual's skills, competency, commitment, and effort. His relationships with others will improve, he will begin to assume additional responsibilities, and will show a willingness to respond in positive ways to change. He will experience a sense of growth, progress, achievement, and job-related satisfaction, and will begin to make reasonable progress toward the best use of his time and talents.

Appropriately implemented training and development renders a service and provides a return on investment to both the company and the individual. The company benefits by having the skills and performance necessary to achieve its immediate and long-range goals. The individual is assured of the opportunity for performance success, security on the present job, and expanded potential.

RELATIONSHIP OF EDUCATION TO PERFORMANCE

More time and money devoted to training may not result in improved skills. More leadership training may not produce better supervision. Don't bet on a direct correlation between amount of formal education and management success. The quantity of learning experience may not always result in improved job performance.

Behavior modification on the job depends on both change in the individual and the job environment that permits the change to occur. Vast sums of money often are wasted in sending individuals to well-conceived, professional, management-type, intracompany programs. The individual is informed, stimulated, and eager to implement the newly acquired skills. But, alas, the boss says, "Forget it. I've heard all that stuff before. My way has been successful in the past. Let's not louse it up now with the nutty ideas of someone who doesn't understand that our business is different." Regardless of the individual's ability and willingness to change, opportunities often depend on certain changes occurring in the department or company. If these do not take place, it is impractical for the individual to make much change.

This problem has led to the concept of organizational development (OD). The premise is that, in order for training and development to become truly effective, the organization must change or develop sufficiently to enable it to occur. Rather than focusing total attention and change on the individual, an equal amount of consideration must be on restructuring and changing the job environment. Otherwise, behavior modification will not achieve its expected potential.

"There is no direct relationship between performance in school or in training programs and records of success in management,"

according to J. Sterling Livingston.[1] In "Myth of the Well-Educated Manager," Dr. Livingston concluded that "grades fail to predict how well an individual will perform in management and that academic success and business achievement have relatively little association with each other." Management development and professional leadership programs emphasize fact gathering, problem solving, and decision making. Little attention is given to finding the problems that need to be solved or the skills necessary for a successful solution as related to final results.

Many professional leadership programs I have personally participated in as a speaker have concentrated on concepts of management, planning, organizing, standards and controls, climate, appraisal, and theories. Negligible attention has been given to the real world of "Will it fly? How can it be implemented—made to work?" Dr. Livingston's research supports the conclusion that education or theoretical training beyond certain levels might have a reverse effect on managerial success. Research and theory can become a crutch, a reason for delay in making decisions and failure to take decisive action. In the real world managers are rewarded and promoted for getting results, which depends on the courage and decisiveness to make the right things happen on a timely basis. In the final analysis, it is not theory, education, or conceptual understanding that advances an individual up the managerial ladder but, rather, a track record of achieved results.

THE ROLE OF TRAINING AND DEVELOPMENT

I have repeatedly cautioned training specialists that a company is not in the training business. Its defined purpose or goal is not engaging in successful training oriented toward producing a well-educated manager. Rather, the proper role of training is to provide a competent staff, and its value must be measured by the contribution it makes to the planned production, sales, service, and profit goals of the company. It should not be an end in itself but a service that enables individuals to make greater contributions in their various positions. If this concept is ignored, the important and necessary function of training becomes diverted into nonproductive activities.

[1] J. Sterling Livingston, "Myth of the Well-Educated Manager," *Harvard Business Review*, January–February 1971.

REQUIREMENTS OF INDIVIDUAL POSITIONS

Specific training and development needs can be gleaned from an examination of position descriptions and standards of performance.

The position description identifies and describes the title and general purpose of the job (what it is supposed to contribute), the specific duties (activities) and responsibilities, accountability and authority (right to take action), and reporting relationship (position to which this position reports and positions reporting to it).

This should provide a reasonable definition of what an individual in this position is required to do. To perform successfully, of course, he or she must possess the qualifications to carry out these duties and responsibilities.

Standards describe the results that will occur when job performance is considered acceptable—in other words, what constitutes acceptable performance based on quantified results. Both the supervisor and the supervised should develop a joint understanding of how well the job is expected to be done. This understanding is based on dollars of sales, percentage of increase, numbers, amount of change, time required, or by what date—objective criteria for setting and judging performance.

The position description provides the "what," and the standards of performance provides the "how well" of the job. When performance results are appraised, it can be determined whether results are under, equal to, or beyond expectation. Any shortcomings should be met through improvement in the performance of the incumbent. The standards often identify clear-cut needs for improvements in performance that can be met through additional training. A thorough analysis of actual job performance and causes for various types of less than satisfactory performance would be required to determine whether training or some other influence might be more appropriate to alter results.

DETERMINING CURRENT AND FUTURE TRAINING NEEDS

The training specialist must look at the total human resource plan and identify gaps, needs, and requirements that could be improved by training. Improvement programs should not be planned or initiated until needs or goals have been accepted. For example:

—Production must increase 10 percent to match a wage increase of 10 percent.
—Eighteen additional supervisors will be needed by January 1 of next year for the new plant.
—Due to retirements and other predictable losses, 15 executive-level replacements will be needed each year.
—In six months a new manufacturing process will begin, requiring production skills not possessed by any of the present workforce.
—A new product will be marketed, beginning July 1.
—The tool manufacturing department will cease operation in two months and the employees will be absorbed in other jobs requiring different skills.
—Forty new employees will be reporting each month who will be unfamiliar with the company and will not possess required productive skills.
—The president has stated that he wants merchandise losses due to dishonesty reduced at least 20 percent by March 1.
—The quality control department has requested help in reducing rejects.
—Employee benefits will be revised, January 1.
—The company wants to initiate a program to improve customer relations.
—The auditing department recommends reducing errors by at least half.

The form in Figure 7 enables a unit manager to identify training needs and communicate those needs by means of a requisition to those concerned with providing the desired training.

Training and development functions can expect to make their greatest contribution to the needs reflected above. They are specific, identified needs that must be met. The identified need for training should be based on company goals as they indicate performance and contribution requirements on the part of individuals. These individuals must possess the necessary competence and be willing to engage in appropriate job activity. Both management

Figure 7. Form to identify company training needs.

TRAINING DEVELOPMENT REQUISITION

Location _____

Division _____

Department _____

Supervisor _____

TRAINING PROGRAMS

1	Basic Development
2	Junior Executive Development
3	Professional Development
4	Management Development
5	AMA Intra-Company Briefing
6	Personnel Practices
7	Individual Management Techniques
8	Organizational Planning
9	Communications
10	Managing Management Time
11	A Univ.-Sponsored Executive Course
12	Financial Training
13	Middle Management Workshop
14	Managers Workshop

DEVELOPMENT SUGGESTIONS

15 16 17 18

AREAS OF DEVELOPMENT NEEDED

Employee's Name

1.
2.
3.
4.
5.
6.
7.
8.
9.
10.

/ - Date Completed   ——— Does not need to do job; X - Needs training.   ☐ Insert date training will be completed and the training specialists should analyze and implement the improvement or growth activities that will enable individuals to meet these needs.

DESIGNING PROGRAMS TO MEET SPECIFIC NEEDS

The fabric of training must be cut to meet the pattern established by the need. It is not my purpose here to cover in detail the endless types of training and development programs available. Educators, consultants, training specialists, and managers have constructed a great variety of skill training and development techniques and programs. National associations of trainers, packaged programs, and a whole industry for producing training aids are making specific contributions to the training function. My concern will be to identify the overall role training and development should make as a vital part of the total human resource plan and to offer some judgments on fully implementing this tool. Development will focus on approaches for improving the individual's capacity to achieve results.

My own experience has been oriented toward designing and budgeting training to reach specific goals. If the individual must sell $42.50 per hour in order to break even, based on pay per hour, then training should be designed and implemented to enable the individual to achieve that goal. If the junior executive trainee is expected to be responsible for certain activities and achieve specified results at the end of one year, then the junior executive development program will fall short if it does not show that trainee how to reach this goal.

Training should start with the result the company expects. Regardless of the type or length of the program involved, it should be oriented toward that goal. Training programs that miss the mark generally do so because they are self-serving rather than realistically directed toward specific company operating results. Programs that are not results-oriented should be altered or dropped. Unless there is an identified result, the program should not be initiated. Programs can and should serve more than the "bottom line" concept; training can also be expected to make specific contributions to other areas such as social, civic, and personal. A company has every legal right to design and direct its training budget and time wherever it chooses, but in all instances this should be done in response to a specific need or goal.

INTERNAL VERSUS EXTERNAL PROGRAMS

Programs and activities conducted for the purpose of improving the current or future job performance of individuals can be either internally or externally arranged.

Internal programs have the advantage of being designed specifically to meet the needs of the company. They generally have the benefit of management participation in their planning, implementation, and continuing visibility as a follow-up. They are usually conducted on company premises during normal work hours, using company equipment and personnel. The program can be altered as quickly and as drastically as changing circumstances require. Those attending have common goals and interests in only one company. The program can be conducted in terms of goals and needs of the company. The program has the backing and support of management. Results should be actionable by both the individual and the group.

Internal programs have the disadvantage of being limited to the skills, knowledge, and expertise available within a single company. Also, the discussion, material covered, and cross polarization afforded by different experiences and points of view are limited to that available in the company. Often, only larger companies can afford the staff specialists desirable for conducting programs of a highly professional quality. Consultants and outside expertise can be employed on a temporary basis, but unless they remain, the ongoing program must be conducted by company personnel. Although company executives are successful managers, they often turn out to be ineffective communicators and teachers. When this is the case, the individual in the program will be inadequately trained and may receive a negative impression of company leadership.

External programs might range from community-sponsored, skills-type programs to university executive programs and professional courses for presidents. They might be conducted during regular work hours, at night, or on weekends. They are often conducted in an educational classroom, motel, or facility provided by the sponsoring organization. The registration fee might vary from no charge to thousands of dollars. Travel and lodging might entail additional cost.

The advantages of participating in outside programs include the availability of highly qualified professional instructors. They might be educators, consultants, or executives who are specialists in a subject area and are experienced as teachers. The program material is generally used repeatedly and tested for effectiveness. Those attending represent a cross section of companies and disciplines, with diversified backgrounds and experiences. The greatest benefit from this type of program might be the input and ideas from other people who are attending—thus providing opportunities for creativity, innovation, and feedback not available within a single company.

Disadvantages might include additional cost and longer periods of time away from the company. It is often difficult to evaluate in advance the contents, value, and applicability of the program. New types of information might confuse the individual. But perhaps the most serious disadvantage is that much of the information requires changes in the way the job is being managed. Since jobs must interact with one another and the company system of goals, controls, and policies, it might not be possible for the returning executive to implement many of the newly acquired ideas.

One major company attempts to make attendance at outside programs more productive by requiring everyone attending to write down five ideas that will be implemented as a result of the program. A copy is sent to the immediate supervisor and to the company president. A follow-up report is required six months later, indicating whether the ideas have been implemented. If ideas have not been implemented, an explanation is required. This type of disciplined follow-up is more likely to result in change than situations left to chance.

TYPICAL RESULT-ORIENTED TRAINING PROGRAMS

Company-structured and -conducted programs should be tailored to promote the achievement of specific goals. The selection of outside programs and instructors should be chosen on the same basis. Return on investment in human resources, including all expenditures for time and resources involved in training and development, should be evaluated by the company as critically as any other expenditure. The following areas represent the major categories of training.

Initial or orientation training for new employees. Every new employee, regardless of level, should have sufficient orientation to allow him or her to mesh smoothly into the human and physical environment of the company. This includes familiarity with compensation and promotional practices, employee benefits, various company practices and policies—in effect, what the individual can expect from the company and what the company expects from the individual.

The new employee cannot be expected to fit into the company and respond satisfactorily to the organization's guidelines and requirements if these are not communicated and understood. Lack of knowledge, lack of comprehension, and misunderstanding about certain guidelines will result in gaps in teamwork between subordinates and supervisors. The company will be dissatisfied if the individual is not fitting in; likewise, the employee can become disgruntled if there is a lack of understanding or acceptance regarding his or her expectations of the company.

Skills training. The purpose of buying the individual's time and presence on the job is the production or contribution that will result. The individual must possess the skills and competencies associated with that position. Skills training must ensure that these fundamentals are possessed to a sufficient degree to enable the individual to perform in a satisfactory manner.

The salesperson can't sell if he or she doesn't understand the techniques of selling. The cashier can't balance the cash if he or she doesn't know how. The heavy equipment operator is both unproductive and dangerous if unskilled in the operation of the equipment. Skills training protects the investment in time on the job; until production is reached, there is a lack of return on investment. Training should provide insurance that return on investment in human time will be achieved.

Supervisory training and development. The performance, attitudes, loyalty, permanence, return on investment, and growth of subordinates are a direct reflection of the quality of supervisory leadership. The investment stakes and return increase proportionately with higher management levels. Every individual's immediate supervisor represents management and company to that individual. The supervisor has a far greater influence on the work life of the subordinate than all other factors combined. The supervisor becomes the key to new forms of motivation as revealed by behavioral scientists—recognition for good work, work relationships, the ability to interact, fuller use of potential, and the provision for individual employee needs.

Serious gaps exist when traditional supervisors, while hardworking and oriented toward getting the work done, are only superficially trained in the delicate skills of human leadership. The typical supervisor was promoted through the ranks and often had no formal training in providing effective leadership for people. The work ethic of the older supervisors was formed prior to World War II, when employees were fortunate to have a job and the motivation for performance was the prospect of unemployment and hunger. Supervisors who were trained in that environment give little attention to the psychological needs and positive versus neutral motivators for employees.

Far more attention should be given to the qualifications and training of supervisors at every level. From the first-line supervisor to the president, leadership's primary job is providing the working framework and direction for people. The untrained supervisor, rather than being a problem solver, becomes a problem creator. Eighty percent of the management-level problems I have been asked to solve should have been handled by the supervisor. Those difficulties that had not been resolved had generally been complicated through mishandling. The crucial link in human resource planning and utilization is the quality of leadership provided by everyone who supervises other people. If supervisors have an appropriate understanding of their roles and possess the skills to carry them out, most of the other factors will tend to fall in place. If they are good trainers, most of the training in the department will be done and production will flow. If they are properly handling the employee relations aspect of their jobs, compensation, benefits, and morale-related factors will be handled in a positive manner. It is at "boss" level for every employee that it happens or fails to happen. If the company wants to identify and focus on the success or failure point, it must give attention to the development of supervisory performance.

Executive development. Executive management must continue to improve its abilities, knowledge, and performance. The internal and external environment changes, problems change, and leadership requirements change. Obsolescence can occur very rapidly in executives who don't exert the effort to keep abreast of current demands and engage in those activities that will ensure their competitive superiority.

Larger companies attempt to design and conduct in-house executive programs. Outside programs are conducted by universities, professional associations such as the American Management Associations, and consultants. They might concentrate on one subject such as communications or transactional analysis, or on a broad range of subjects covering the various functional areas of management. These programs have been constructive in elevating the performance level and the practice of management. They have enabled management to keep tuned in on what's occurring in the various fields of management and to substantially increase the professional level of management. They have also improved the skills needed in functional areas—planning, organizing, coordinating, controlling, motivating, and results appraisal.

In designing and seeking training programs to meet specific company needs, critical ROI testing should occur. In an American Management Associations Survey report, Dr. Robert F. Pearse found that most managers considered on-the-job experience their most important source of training and development. He found that most managers question the real value of management-type programs. However, managers did feel that they had benefited from the recent findings of behavioral scientists regarding areas of motivation and human behavior.[2]

Special duties and assignments. The use of special assignments as a development tool often benefit both the company and the individual. These assignments might involve being a member of a group or having sole responsibility for an activity. Typical are appointment as a member of a special committee, assignment to a special project, job rotation, filling in for another executive, serving

[2] Robert F. Pearse, *Manager to Manager—What Managers Think of Management Development,"* AMACOM, 1974.

on standing committees, and providing constructive input for special problems confronted by management.

Special management development areas might also include computer assignments, problem simulation and solution, management games, and a wide variety of techniques and tools devised to enable management to measure executive competency and predict future potential. Research is constantly going forward in finding ways to predict management success and in developing managerial skills. Mistakes are costly for both the company and the individual; thus the pursuit for increased certainty of success continues.

MEASURING NEED FOR INDIVIDUAL GROWTH

In the final analysis, the impact from training and development should be on the performance and potential of individuals. After company needs have been identified, they should be translated into individual growth needs. This is done by identifying and classifying deficiencies in qualifications and performance, reaching an understanding on what the employee, supervisor, and the company will do to overcome diagnosed weaknesses, and communicating to all concerned what action will be taken to ensure development. All available training and development resources for the individual's development should be used to motivate the individual to respond fully to all available development opportunities.

The most commonly used technique for identifying individual growth needs is comparison of current job performance with expectations. Is it short of, equal to, or superior to expectations? Which areas offer the greatest opportunities for improvements? What are the factors limiting the individual's promotional opportunities? In its simplest form, this is a judgment—preferably based on objective facts of how well the individual is currently performing.

Once these needs for improvement and growth have been identified and measured, a training opportunity emerges. The manager should aggressively seek to meet the opportunity through personal training, coaching, and company-initiated programs. One company uses the joint-venture approach of measuring and providing opportunities for improvement. The program identifies current performance level and potential but concentrates its greatest effort on

Figure 8. Profile to identify training and development needs for individual executives.

Name _____

Based on the appraisal of performance and/or the appraisal of potential for the above-named employee, it is the opinion of the two of us (rater and ratee) that training and development could be helpful in the areas checked.

PERSONAL SKILLS

_____ Written expression, letters, reports, instructions, etc.

_____ Oral presentations, use of visual aids.

_____ Reading improvement.

_____ Communication techniques, listening.

_____ Conference leadership.

_____ Problem solving, logic.

_____ Creative thinking.

_____ Human relations.

_____   _____

_____   _____

EMPLOYEE RELATIONS

_____ Employee utilization.

_____ Company personnel policies and practices.

_____ Interviewing, selection.

_____ Performance appraisals.

_____ Techniques for training subordinates.

_____ Management development.

_____   _____

_____   _____

SUPERVISORY SKILLS

_____ Work and employee scheduling.

_____ Motivation.

_____ Delegation.

_____ Budgeting.

_____ Statistics, reports, records.

_____ Use of computerized information.

_____   _____

_____   _____

MANAGEMENT SKILLS

_____   Company organization and functions.

_____   Line and staff relationships.

_____   Company policies.

_____   Planning, one-year goals.

_____   Planning, five-year goals.

_____   Cost control.

_____   Decision making.

_____   Government regulations.

_____   _____

_____   _____

What do you and the employee agree are needed for preparedness in his or her career?

a. Skills development _____

b. Specialized training _____

c. Broadening experience, maybe job rotation _____

d. Exposure outside the company _____

e. Other _____

At this time, how does the employee qualify for the next higher position?

a. Is the employee ready now? Explain _____

b. Can the employee be made ready soon? Explain _____

c. Does the employee understand what must occur in order to earn more money and/or be promoted? _____

Are there any conditions or considerations that would have an effect on the employee's career plan or future (age, health, family circumstances, transferable, etc.)?

_____

_____

_____

Prepared by _____   _____

(Manager)   (Date)

In consultation with _____   _____

(Employee)   (Date)

Reviewed by _____   _____

(Personnel or Training Officer of Unit)   (Date)

future opportunities for growth rather than on past failures. The supervisor and the employee discuss and agree jointly on areas where growth opportunities exist. Working together, they agree on specific activities to ensure that opportunities will be realized. Each accepts an equal share of the responsibility for a constructive approach to improving both current performance and future potential.[3] Figure 8 is a checklist to help identify the training and development needs for individual executives.

INDIVIDUAL CAREER PROGRAMMING

In recent years increased attention has been given to planning and managing individual careers. Terms such as "career charting," "career mapping," "career planning," and "individual career management" are being used to describe individual career planning. A flood of articles in professional publications and a book by Marion S. Kellogg [4] have called attention to this important facet of human resource planning.

Essentially, individual career planning is the other side of the human resource planning coin. The company typically focuses its planning activity on ensuring that needed human resources will be available. The goal is providing for company needs. Individual career planning provides for the career-achievement needs of the individual.

The reasons most often given by bright, ambitious, career-oriented individuals for leaving a company center around better opportunity elsewhere. The better opportunity might not exist in the other company; in fact, the better opportunity is often in the present company. Then why do major companies lose up to half their management trainees during their first two years of employment? The problem is principally one of communication, understanding, and adequate planning on the part of both the company and the individual. Both must share the responsibility for planning and managing careers.

Companies have traditionally missed the target by a wide margin in determining needs, in knowing what accounts for success

---

[3] Ray A. Killian, *The Working Woman—A Male Manager's View,* AMACOM, 1971, p. 97.

[4] Marion S. Kellogg, *Career Management,* AMACOM, 1972.

and through sponsoring promotional-utilization programs in which too much waste is built into the program. If the company acquires more physical facilities than it needs, some will not be fully utilized. If the company employs more people than needed, or fails to provide growth opportunity, not all will be fully utilized and some employees will leave for better opportunity elsewhere. In some instances companies have overestimated; in others underplanning has occurred and outside recruitment is necessary.

The whole system of company and career management should be overhauled if both the needs of the company and the career aims of the individual are to be realized. Individual career management consists of the following essential factors:

1. An individual career portfolio designed to incorporate all needed career planning information.

2. Personal information: education, work history, skills, experience, and personal factors that might bear on career pathing.

3. Records of job performance—how well the individual has performed on jobs to date.

4. Aptitude and career interests as expressed by the individual and as indicated by interest tests and observations of supervisors.

5. An appraisal of potential and probable course of success as indicated by individual and management evaluation.

6. Availability of the individual for promotion and, possibly, willingness to relocate geographically.

7. In-depth analysis of strengths and weaknesses revealed by job performance evaluation as they might relate to current performance and future career paths.

8. A jointly developed plan and commitment by both the individual and the company regarding development programs that will be most constructive.

9. The mapping of an individually tailored career, including probable positions and dates.

10. The commitment of resource and time for career achievement on the part of both the individual and the company.

It should be recognized that although most progressive companies are engaged in mapping and implementing successful career management, responsibility also rests with the individual. The right of self-determination should remain that of the individual, and he or she should assume the initiative for the management of his or her own career. However, when this becomes a joint effort, both company and employee increase their chances of achieving mutually desirable goals.

The joint-venture approach enables the company to plan and operate its business. It permits the individual to plan a career based on his or her assessment of his or her own education, qualifications, interests, and commitment.

In its planning process, the company identifies the various career opportunities available currently and in the future. It seeks to link individual career goals to company goals by providing various developmental guides and programs to enable the individual to reach career goals while filling the company's needs. This system will work best if both the individual and the company understand the proper role each will assume in career charting and success. The company must make opportunities available and must also provide the framework for the achievement of individual career goals. This involves all areas of training and development, evaluation of job performance, promotional systems, and a meshing of company and individual goals. The individual must be willing to participate in those programs and activities, both internally and externally, that are most likely to lead to career success. In doing so, he or she must produce the type of batting averages that will cause management to promote him or her to higher levels of career success. Optimum results will not occur unless there is constant, effective communication and a candid understanding between company and individual.

The relationship of superior and subordinate emerges as the key to the career stairway. Focus should be on intermediate jobs and ultimate job, strengths and limitations, gaps, and options for development. Goals should be realistic and attainable. Practical dates should be accepted. Initial and continuing attention should be given to motivation for ambitious career pursuit.

The successful mapping and management of individual careers will be the key to meeting the company's vital need for capable management. Increasingly, individuals will insist on the right to determine where they will work and what they will do in connection with their careers. Career interests and planning will become more highly individualized and less historically stereotyped. The company's success in attracting, motivating, and retaining needed leadership will depend on the quality of its career systems. Unless the company is able to demonstrate a philosophy and practice of concern for individual career interests, aggressive, career-oriented people will go elsewhere.

How well does the career system work? The individual will be influenced more by the fact of what is happening than by what the company says should be happening. What do the career paths and history of people in the company reveal? What is the company doing by way of professional development and growth to enable individuals to advance their careers? What have been the promotional practices? Have better positions been filled from the outside? Are the pattern and practice likely to provide the type of career opportunity being sought by the individual? Companies must accept the fact that people are intelligent—if they have been oversold on career opportunities, they will soon find out. If their needs are not met, they will leave.

INTERACTION OF TRAINING WITH INTERNAL AND EXTERNAL FORCES

Here are some of the issues that need to be considered when training and development plans are being made.

1. What structures and new processes the competitive environment will require the organization to develop to cope with change.

2. The many jobs and skills that will become obsolete and have to be replaced.

3. The balance between meeting the needs of the company and the career interests of the individual as they relate to development and the maximum utilization of human potential.

4. The growing emphasis training programs must place on individual creativity and innovation as related to job performance and career growth.

5. Training and development that enable individuals to become a more meaningful, interactive part of the company and to use the full potential of their mind and talents.

6. Programs that will equip both manager and employee to cope with conflict, confrontation, openness, and two-way feedback.

7. The knowledge and technology explosion must be channeled

and appropriately utilized for the mutual benefit of company and individual.

8. Training and development that will assume an increased role for the performance and career growth of underutilized groups —blacks, women, and others.

9. The achievement of improved performance rather than increased knowledge.

10. Assignment of specific accountability to all supervisors for implementing training and development.

11. Greater insistence on ROI goal-oriented evaluation of all training activities and expenses instead of assuming results based on promises or faith.

MEASURING ROI COSTS AND RESULTS

Money spent for plants and raw material creates a productive capacity. Interest paid on capital makes needed financial resources available. But what benefit does the company receive for the dollars spent for training materials, staffs, films, consultants, employee attendance at outside programs, and time spent by line executives in training activities? The expense and time devoted to training will be accepted only when this activity has developed objective criteria for proving its beneficial impact on company goals.

Increasingly, companies are using scientific and research approaches to measure training results. Test or control groups are used to measure the contribution of training. Does the increase in production and sales justify the amount of training expense? Have programs actually caused modifications in behavior? Are the individuals who have participated in either in-house or outside executive programs more effective, and are they promotable faster? What is the immediate and long-range impact?

When only one part of the job improves, it is difficult to evaluate the future value or overall performance of training. The program should be measured during and at the completion of training. If goals have not been achieved, reasons should be discovered. Was the program content or the trainers at fault? Were the wrong people sent to the program? Was the participant unable to apply training results in his or her department? Did unanticipated internal or external changes occur?

Companies without well-defined improvement programs will find it increasingly difficult to attract and retain capable leaders. Without the capacity for updating skills and utilizing latest knowledge and techniques, the company will cease to be competitive. Training and development are key tools available to management for maximizing human resource performance, career growth, and ROI. But in order to be effective, training must be built deep into the company systems, involving all layers of management and affecting the way the enterprise works. It must be part of every manager's position description and standard of performance and accountability. Top management support and commitment must be unwavering; otherwise, formalized human development will stop.

9
Maximizing
human productivity

Productivity has been called the key to the economic health of every company. It is a gauge of how well the company operates internally, determined by measuring cost against output. When compared with similar companies in the same type of industry, productivity becomes the competitive bench mark for survival. National productivity determines the ultimate cost of goods and services as compared with those produced in other countries.

The whole human resource return on investment concept comes to rest squarely on the foundation of productivity. What is the market value of goods and services produced by the company's human resources as compared with the cost involved? When costs exceed produced value, the company loses money. When costs of human time or other factors rise faster than production, the continuity of the business becomes uncertain. Unless reserves are available, or unless the imbalance can be corrected, eventually the company will exhaust resources and cease to operate.

Within the legal and ethical framework existing, owners must make decisions regarding what is a fair profit and what portion of productivity results should be shared with employees. Also to be considered in deciding on what amounts to be shared are reserves or reinvestment amounts that will be made in the company for research, new or improved facilities, and expanded markets. My position, as stated at various points in this book, is that there should be equitable sharing of contribution and productivity results.

Appropriate corporate planning and operation should bring about an acceptable level of productivity. Planning should provide for a fair return to investors, the payment of taxes and financial obligations, amounts for reinvestments in the future of the business, and a meaningful sharing of productivity results with employees through direct compensation, benefits, and a profit sharing.

INFLUENCES ON PRODUCTIVITY

The powerful influences of government, unions, and modern lifestyles make sharing of contribution a requirement for the effort and productivity of employees. When the job does not provide for the individual's needs—recognition, opportunity, pay, appropriate leadership—in relation to input, productivity efforts fail. The attitude becomes: "My effort and production don't really make any difference in what I receive from my job, so why go all out? I can get by just as well by doing only what is required. It's not my job to improve what's being done. Let the bosses do it—that's what they're getting paid to do. They don't really appreciate help from anyone else." Thus the thrust for profitable productivity, sought through elaborate company planning and industrial engineering, fails to materialize.

In a Survey Report to AMA members, Mildred E. Katzell reported respondents' evaluations of the influence of various factors on productivity (see Table 2). Ultimately, productivity hinges on the company's overall effectiveness in meriting contribution by individual employees. This key to productivity receives far too little attention and commitment from corporate management.

PRODUCTIVITY:
THE MAJOR COMPETITIVE BATTLEGROUND

According to another AMA Survey Report of over 1,200 corporate presidents and executives—

During a recent ten-year period productivity gains in the United States were the lowest in the world.

—About 50 to 70 percent of the U.S. workforce is underutilized.

Table 2. Percent of respondents considering each factor as "very important" or as "unimportant" in terms of influencing the Organization's productivity.

	VERY IMPORTANT	UNIMPORTANT *
Better planning	66	2
More effective management	65	4
Improved job procedures	49	7
Improved communications	48	9
More recognition for achievement	45	10
Better training of employees	45	8
More management attention to productivity	39	11
Better human relations	36	13
Improved technology	35	23
New ways to motivate workers	34	17
Increased market demand	31	32
Changes in government regulations	30	38
Greater capital investment	27	23
Harder work by employees	25	20
More employee loyalty	23	24
Greater union cooperation	22	42
More opportunities for advancement	18	25
Improved quality of working life	16	27
Improved working conditions	16	34
Job redesign and enlargement	12	44
Greater participation by workers in decision making	10	49
More worker incentive programs	10	52
More democracy in the organization	6	64
More competition among companies	6	67
Better transportation to work	4	83

* "Not Very Important" and "Not at All Important" combined.
Source: Mildred E. Katzell, *Productivity: The Measure and the Myth,* AMACOM, 1975.

—Sixty percent of the U.S. workforce is now white-collar, and 70 percent of this group could produce significantly more.[1]
—Ninety-six percent of the survey respondents believe that improved productivity in all personnel areas would help accomplish

[1] Herman S. Jacobs and Katherine Jillson, *Executive Productivity,* AMACOM, 1974, p. 5.

organizational goals such as improvement in profit, return on investment, product quality, or ability to attract capital.

—Sixty-three percent of the respondents say that executive productivity is a "serious concern" in the operation of business and industry today.[2]

Changing Times reported that—

A lot of very competent experts say that productivity is the key to most of our economic and social concerns—to cure such ills as unemployment, inflation, and weak profits, and to the achievement of such goals as general prosperity, a satisfactory balance of payments, better housing, better living standards, even a strong stock market . . . a nation with a sagging productivity is a nation in trouble.[3]

Although the U.S. worker is still the most productive in the world, the competitive edge has been constantly eroded during recent years. Gains in some nations of Europe and Asia have outpaced U.S. workers up to sixfold. (See Table 3.)

Number of jobs, job security, and individual opportunity are dependent on the productivity of the company, as compared with other companies, and how well the price and quality of its goods

Table 3. Average annual productivity gain of U.S. worker compared with workers in other countries. [4]

COUNTRY	1965–1970	1970–1972
United States	2.0%	4.9%
United Kingdom	3.9	6.6
Canada	4.7	5.1
Italy	5.3	3.5
Germany	5.7	5.1
France	6.0	6.9
Sweden	7.7	4.5
Belgium	7.9	6.5
Netherlands	8.9	6.6
Japan	13.2	7.7

[2] Ibid., p. 2.

[3] Copyright 1975, *Changing Times,* The Kiplinger Magazine, Washington, D.C., February 1974, p. 47.

[4] Ibid.

and services stack up when compared with imports. The competitive value of productivity is the ultimate basis for growth or demise of companies and individual opportunities. Therefore, the real battleground or crux of all human resource planning must focus on productivity.

Productivity is the most serious challenge confronting management leadership. Since it is the key to the internal profitability of the company and the best measure of its external competitiveness, the future of the company rests heavily on productivity result. Management must constantly confront all challenges associated with the market value of what the company produces as compared with the total cost of producing it. The margin between cost and price determines profit, available funds for reinvestment, company growth, and future opportunity for employees.

UNDERSTANDING AND MEASURING HUMAN PRODUCTIVITY

Human time is the most costly ingredient in the majority of the goods and services produced in the United States. Raw materials, capital, buildings, machines, and markets are generally available on an equal basis to companies. The competitive edge as represented by lower-cost production and a better-value product is principally the human ingredient. The human production ingredient takes the form of human organization, competency, and effort. It consists of the productivity opportunity made available by the company and the response contribution made by individual employees at all levels.

Productivity can best be understood by analyzing the balance of factors that affect the conversion of resources into useful products and services. The many costs to be considered would include all those items necessary to bring the production facilities to a state of readiness and purchase of the raw material to be converted into a marketable item. The principal additional cost in bringing about the conversion and the added value represented is human time. The biggest cost question then becomes the amount of human time involved and the cost of that time for each unit of product or service.

The company must constantly seek better ways to improve production cost and the market value of what has been produced. A reason for concern is that approximately 80 percent of factory production jobs are covered by performance standards, but only 5 percent of white-collar workers are covered. It has been estimated that administrative employee performance is only 60 percent effective—40 percent wasted. As composition of the total workforce shifts to a higher percentage of white-collar and administrative employees, major attention must be focused on finding and implementing more efficient ways for the use of time and talent of employees to reduce the cost of human time required for production. In most instances the cost of human time per hour, as expressed in direct compensation and employee benefits, is constantly increasing. Therefore, in order to maintain or increase production per dollar of human time cost, new forms of technology, automation, systems improvement, and increased employee competency and effort must be achieved. It is unwise to assume that any one of these areas will produce the desired results. Rather, maximum results are dependent on improvement of all productive efforts.

BENEFITS OF WORK MEASUREMENT

Work measurement is essential if cost is to be compared with output. Benefits of work measurement include better control of work scheduling and assignment of work, improved service and reduced time for processing, more efficient budgeting and use of human resources, more accurate setting of priorities, a basis for evaluating change, a basis for evaluating job performance, and factual information for future decisions and action.

Management, supervisors, and employees should have a clear understanding of the productivity index. Productivity is the measure of how much can be done or made in a given period, measured against what went into the task. When the same amount can be produced in less time, productivity has been increased. It is from the leftover margin that the company meets its obligations to stockholders, future reinvestments in the company, and sharing with employees.

Table 4. Extent of agreement with statements explaining productivity.

	PERCENT AGREEING
1. Productivity means *quality* of output as well as *quantity*.	95
2. Productivity refers to the output per man-hour in any one company or organization.	90
3. Productivity means the overall efficiency and effectiveness of the operation.	88
4. Productivity includes such intangibles as disruptions, "shrinkage," sabotage, and other indicators of trouble in the organization, even when their impact on output cannot be measured easily.	73
5. Productivity includes such factors as rate of absenteeism and turnover as measures of output.	70
6. Productivity includes measures of customer or client satisfaction.	64
7. Productivity includes such intangibles as employee loyalty, morale, and job satisfaction.	55
8. Productivity refers to the ratio of output to input by industry or section of the economy, not by individual organization.	22

Source: Mildred E. Katzell, *Productivity: The Measure and the Myth,* AMACOM, 1975.

Total productivity is difficult to measure, since valid figures depend on accurate means of measuring every input cost. This usually takes the form of prorating to each unit such factors as cost of machinery, raw materials, transportation, labor, overhead, management, and many others. Cost accounting methods attempt to allocate these figures accurately.

The survey results reported in Table 4 reveal the understanding respondents had regarding productivity. Note the majority agreement on the top five factors.

IMPACT OF PRODUCTIVITY

The vital impact of productivity on the company and its basic goals and results should focus attention on increasing productivity.

Human efforts are generally concentrated in areas of training, supervision, communications, motivation, and various factors influencing the competency and efforts of individual employees. Of equal concern should be the employee's productivity opportunity, as influenced by the efficiency of the physical environment and human climate in which he works. In many instances the individual's productivity is significantly influenced by factors beyond his control. It is generally the company that controls the tools and machinery, the raw material, and the systems of production.

Human productivity should be concerned with measuring human cost in all areas of the company, although this is difficult and especially tedious in nonproduction and service areas. It is easier to measure cost of units produced on the assembly line than productivity of an accountant in a large office. It is simpler to determine the cost of selling in a department store than the cost of management for each dollar of sales. Actual measurement of human cost input, as accurately allocated to the unit cost of every product or service, is one of the most difficult in determining a fair productivity cost.

But the use of computers and improved cost accounting methods have narrowed margins of error in allocating costs, and total human costs are becoming more realistic by including in addition to direct compensation and benefits, cost of employment, turnover, training, and other factors as part of the cost of human time. Of principal concern is finding a fair basis for determining the actual cost of production, a quantitative system for establishing compensation, a mutually acceptable basis for communicating job expectations, and an accurate means for analyzing results of job performance.

In addition, both unions and government have a direct concern with productivity. The union seeks to obtain a reasonable share of productivity results for employees through pay, benefits, and working conditions. If compensation levels, as a share of productivity, are unsatisfactory to the union, restrictions on production are imposed, limiting the number of bricks laid per hour or the number of units produced per day. This ploy seeks to protect or increase the number of jobs and obtain a larger share of each unit of production. This—in conjunction with requirements for premium pay (double and triple time) additional benefits, and other employee expenses—increases the cost of production and narrows the gap between cost of input and value of output. Also, various government regulations impose such expense-adding factors as equal pay, safety regulations, and the employment of less-qualified individuals. Although these requirements might be desirable from a humanistic point of view, they can add to the cost of production. The chairman of the board of Springs Mills stated in a public meeting that the cost of reducing the noise level in the mills to meet the Occupational Safety and Health Act requirements would cost $28 million, without producing one additional inch of fabric. This is typical of the constantly additive costs of production that tend to offset advances in technology.

Increasing costs of human time, production restrictions, and government regulations, as well as the changing lifestyles of employees, have forced companies to pursue all possible avenues for increasing human productivity. This must be done within the frameworks of humanistic, social, and government acceptability. But the fact remains that companies still have available excellent, unutilized opportunities for improving productivity by reducing absenteeism, improving training, providing a higher quality of leadership, offering more appropriate customer service, engaging in more professional management, planning more accurately, and using the total time and talents of employees more effectively.

GAUGING PRODUCTIVE OPPORTUNITY

As a productivity factor, management should analyze the quality of opportunities available to the individual employee. What constraints versus unlimited opportunities are available? What limitations versus production stimulators does the system impose on less-measurable jobs? A significant step toward analyzing and improving productivity should be that of gauging actual company-provided opportunity. The following is a checklist for measuring opportunity.

Production machinery and tools. Are they as modern and efficient as those being used by others doing similar work throughout the world? (Today, overseas companies also have to be considered.)

Physical arrangement of the work environment. Is it arranged in the most efficient manner, or does it restrict production?

Processes, work flow, and work procedures. How long has it been since they have been analyzed and improved? How do they compare with those of similar industries? Have all processes been rigorously subjected to work simplification and efficiency testing?

Competency of employees. What is the level of their knowledge and skills as related to their ability to produce? Does the quality of goods and services demonstrate that the employees possess an acceptable degree of competency?

Motivational and commitment level of employees. Does the quantity produced show that individuals are committing full effort to the job?

Leadership. What do employee production, turnover, dissatisfaction, attendance, morale, and overall job relationship demonstrate concerning the quality of leadership?

Conditions of raw material, markets, and other productive elements. Is the condition and quality of raw material conducive to efficient conversion to an added-value product? Have markets been enhanced through favorable company reputation and advertising?

Quantity and quality of the human resources available. Is the amount of human time purchased too much or too little? The purchase of surplus time will result in lowered productivity per man-hour. Underqualified employees will result in reduced output.

Maximum utilization of all human time and talent. How much time and talent are underutilized or completely wasted? What can be done to maximize productive contribution?

Company attitude and practices. Does the company demonstrate a genuine concern for employees as evidenced by pay and compensation practices, personnel policies, working conditions, and total employee relations? Does the overall program stimulate a maximum productive effort?

Opportunity to perform the work. This involves having sufficient information, authority needed to proceed, skills required, clear understanding of job scope, support of supervisor and associates, and confidence to perform without undue fear of harsh criticism.

In their effort to improve production, many companies make

the serious mistake of admonishing their employees to work harder. It should be assumed that employees want to do a good job, that given a reasonable opportunity and understanding of the personal benefits of favorable job results they will put forth their best efforts. Then why isn't this occurring? In most instances, there is a plausible reason—one that often the company controls and can correct.

Gauging productive opportunity implies analyzing why production is not occurring to a satisfactory degree, deciding what should be done to correct it, and implementing the corrective measures. The productive influences, based on the above list, indicate that a significant number of production controls are in the hands of the company and not the employee. It is certainly true that the employee must bring certain input to production such as presence on the job, response to training opportunities, adherence to company guides, and interaction with supervision. But the fact remains that the company, through its control and influence on production factors, retains a significant responsibility for final results. It is the responsibility of the company to structure and implement its various personnel-related programs to maximize human productivity.

EXAMINING PRODUCTIVE EFFECTIVENESS

Efforts to increase production have most often focused solely on physical engineering. This is certainly the area in which the most dramatic change and progress have occurred. Machines and processes, computer and electronic advances, and new technology have provided most of the productive gains during recent years. The selling price of electronic calculators dropped from $1,495 to approximately $50 with the discovery of a tiny chip equivalent to 1,000 transistors, thus reducing the assembly time to as little as 15 minutes. Instances of similar breakthroughs could be repeated hundreds of times, but nothing of a comparable nature has occurred in the human arena. The advances in human skills, education, and motivation have been slow, tedious, and erratic. Claimed panaceas continue to come along, but few have had lasting or major effect on human production. A General Motors vice-president observed that "advances during the next 50 years would be greatest in the area of human factors, because so little has been achieved up to this point."

What is the efficiency of the human resource organization and what influence does it have on production? Human organization is concerned with lines of authority, individual duties and responsibilities, and the general allocation of work to be done by all individuals. Efficient production also relates to department size, span of management control, and the relationship of employee and management. The key to organizational efficiency is whether individuals at every level are given a full and challenging workload and whether the total human environment is conducive to productivity.

Increased organizational size has created its own set of problems. Centralization of authority and control often lessen initiative and innovation. But complete local autonomy could deny the expertise-type benefits available through central management guidance. Each company should seek to achieve that balance between centralized versus local control that will result in the most efficient human organization. Research and comparative results can provide guidelines regarding most effective degree of and point of control.

Regardless of whether formal or informal, the human organization should be structured to provide the greatest productive efficiency. Lack of an effective human structure can result in extreme waste and lack of efficiency. Management must be as deliberate and systematic in planning for the human organization as it is in planning for the physical and production facilities of the company.

INDIVIDUAL COMPETENCY

Can the individual do the job? How long will it take? How accurately is it being done? These questions relate to individual productive competency. Acceptable productivity will not occur unless the individual possesses a sufficient degree of competency. If we assume that the company is providing the maximum productive opportunity by making available appropriate facilities and organization, then the actual input depends on human competency. One expert stated that most unsatisfactory work occurs because the employee simply doesn't know how to do the job or how the company wants it done. It is certain that if the employee doesn't possess the ability to do the required work, or if there is a lack of understanding of what the company will consider satisfactory, then acceptable productivity will not occur. If the company has done its part in providing productive opportunity, then attention should be given to the competency level of individuals.

How much can production be increased on the assembly line by improving the skills and techniques of the assembler? How many errors can be eliminated by the bookkeeper by improving knowledge of accounting and office machine usage? How many dollars can be added to sales by refining the sales techniques of salespeople? Self-concepts of competency reinforce self-assurance and lead to even greater productivity. Ability thus makes possible initial achievement and provides stimulation for repetitive efforts leading to increased results.

EMPLOYEE MOTIVATION

Motivation poses the simple challenge: How can employees be stimulated to put forth their best effort? This is the most complexing challenge confronting the modern American productive system. There appears to be a general feeling on the part of management that all production problems could be solved if every employee had the right work ethic and were fully motivated. The search for solutions to the problem of motivation has led to experimentation in job enrichment, redesign of jobs, and input from behaviorists. Lists of various types of motivators have been developed. Consultants and internal specialists have developed complete programs for stimulating job effort. However, the option for maximum individual effort or lack of effort remains the most significant production uncertainty. The importance of the human will to work might be best emphasized by posing the following questions:

What types of changes and results would occur if every employee in the company put forth his absolute best effort?

What would be the result if a self-activating generator could be implanted in every employee?

Suppose every employee worked like the track star does to win the race and strained as hard to be first to break the ribbon?

Suppose employees exhibited the same degree of interest and achieved the same level of satisfaction from their jobs as that derived from hobbies and recreation?

What would the result be if the gap between potential performance and actual performance were substantially reduced?

If this level of effort and commitment could be sustained, companies—and the world—would never be the same again. What is the mystery? Why doesn't the employee understand that everything he or she wants in connection with the job is more likely to come along if maximum effort is put forth? The company system claims that the more the employee produces the more he or she will be paid, that better performance leads to increased job security, that better work leads to increased recognition and praise, and that improved overall performance leads to improved opportunity for progress and promotion. Why then isn't performance an outpouring of total effort? Many experts believe that full effort is withheld because the employee fails to understand the relationship of contribution to personal gain or because the individual is skeptical of management's willingness to fulfill its claims.

Much of this gap can be eliminated through broad-based involvement by all personnel. Involvement results when management says, "I think you have something important to offer; you are an important, responsible person; your help is needed; and your ideas will be given full consideration." To say this means communicating fully all goals, objectives, and work methods—those for the company, the department, the supervisor, and the individual. It means encouraging each person to set personal objectives relevant to time, production amounts, and costs, and working jointly with employees to develop a work plan of action. It means measuring progress, providing feedback, coaching employees to direct their energies into more productive channels, and helping each person capitalize on strengths and correct the limitations that block his effectiveness. Finally, it means establishing employee relations programs that are designed to improve work attitudes.

The results of an AMA survey (see Table 5) showed certain prevailing views regarding employee attitudes and motivation. The survey found that there was less consensus on these factors than on other areas influencing productivity.

Table 5. Percent holding prevailing views regarding approaches to improving employee attitudes and motivation.

APPROACHES	VERY USEFUL	NOT AT ALL USEFUL
1. Better communication from management	55	1
2. More feedback to employees on how well they are doing	45	1
3. More opportunities for advancement	31	1
4. Better training and education programs	29	2
5. Building loyalty to the organization	28	2
6. Better treatment by supervisors	27	2
7. Sharing of profits or productivity gains	25	4
8. More interesting and challenging work	23	1
9. Greater employee participation	21	2
10. More opportunities for employees to socialize with each other	2	22

Source: Mildred E. Katzell, *Productivity: The Measure and the Myth,* AMACOM, 1975.

Management has the responsibility of understanding fully what motivates employees—what they actually need and want in connection with their jobs. Once this need has been identified, the relationship of expectation and achievement must be communicated to employees in such a manner that they accept the challenge and respond by contributing full effort.

If productivity is the key to return on investment in human resources, then motivated effort is the decisive ingredient of productivity. If there is to be an acceptable rate of return, a high level of motivation must exist in the total workforce. It should be emphasized that everything stated concerning productivity and motivation applies with equal validity to the beginning-level employee up through top management.

Company motivational efforts and programs are generally concentrated in the following areas.

Traditional motivational practices. This is loosely defined as the reward-and-punishment or carrot-and-stick approach. Its primary thrust is leading the individual to an understanding that there is a direct relationship between job effort and contribution to compensation, job security, opportunity, and other benefits that he or she might desire from the company. Company systems and supervisory efforts concentrate on showing and communicating the validity of this relationship. For instance, where companies put forth any real motivational effort, it is most commonly concentrated in this type of motivation. It is often the only type of motivation that supervisors are familiar with and the only type they are trained to implement.

The motivation–hygiene system. Dr. Frederick Herzberg and his associates have been the chief exponents of this approach to understanding motivation. This concept states that certain job influences provide only hygienic satisfaction and that they often become job dissatisfiers. These include company policy and administration, supervision, interpersonal relations, working conditions, salary, status, and security. The motivators that provide positive job satisfaction are achievement, recognition for achievement, the work itself, responsibility, advancement, and growth.[5] Dr. Herzberg states that hygienic factors can be counted on only as temporary motivators, and that they often prove to be the chief source of job complaints. Reputable companies are expected to provide fair pay and reasonable working conditions; therefore, they receive very little favorable credit from the employee for meeting expectation. However, if the company fails to provide positive leadership, job security, appropriate policies and administration, and acceptable working conditions, these influences will result in negative motivation.

The job satisfiers of achievement, recognition, and growth provide for the self-actualization of the individual and permanent types of motivation as long as the climate is maintained. Dr. Herzberg's use of the motivation profile established the classic or normal profile, and when deviations occur, motivational problems can be identified. Of the newer motivational theories, the motivation-hygiene profile has the greatest number of adherents and seems to be experiencing the greatest sustained success.

[5] Frederick Herzberg, "Motivation Hygiene Profiles," *Organizational Dynamics,* Fall 1974.

Job enrichment. Herzberg, Ford at AT&T, and others found that the job itself is capable of providing a valid source of satisfaction, challenge, and motivation for the individual.[6] An enriched job is characterized in these ways:

—It is a complete piece of work where the same individual is involved throughout the process from beginning to end.

—The job incumbent has as much decision-making control over his or her work activities as possible. Decision making is delegated down to the lowest level at which reasonable decision making can be made.

—The individual receives candid, frequent, and direct feedback on performance. Motivation and reinforcement are achieved because the employee always sees his progress and results. The golfer knows every time he hits the ball how well he is doing and how the result will affect the final score. No one else has to tell the person how well he is performing.

—The individual has opportunity for reasonable innovation in deciding how the job will be done and determining what results will be acceptable. The individual wants to feel that he has some direct influence on results and that his input, both mental and physical, makes a significant difference.

—The incumbent has an opportunity to interact with associates and supervisor. Humans are highly gregarious creatures, and they experience a sense of frustration and negativism when isolated from others. Enrichment of job activity involves meaningful association with others in the job environment.

Effective job enrichment should benefit the company through increased productivity, reduced turnover, decreased absenteeism, improved morale and reduction of errors, customer complaints, and costs. The employee benefits through a more interesting job, greater responsibility and opportunity, more effective utilization of skills, quicker recognition for results, accelerated growth and development, improved self-esteem, and more compensation.

Job enrichment is inhibited until certain changes are made. Enrichment requires that decision-making authority must be delegated further down the scale of job levels. Supervisors must be willing to relinquish some of their traditional authority and job

[6] Robert N. Ford, *Motivation Through the Work Itself*, AMACOM, 1969.

control. Companies must be willing to place more trust and confidence in the good intent and intelligence of employees. Job enrichment moves from the highly engineered division of labor—which tends to isolate the task and individual and simplify them to the point of near automation—to a fuller use of the minds and talents of individuals. When the company vertically loads or builds a higher order of responsibility and authority and more challenging content into the job, the individual experiences the satisfaction of achievement, recognition, and growth that makes the job a satisfying, meaningful experience at which he or she is motivated to perform well.

Job redesign. Although similar to job enrichment, which largely involves job influences, job redesign is concerned with the basic nature of the work being done. Many jobs involve tedious, boring, routine processes and details that can be either eliminated entirely or at least redesigned and integrated with other processes to make for a more interesting job.

One management writer has asked, "Are jobs fit for people?" Peter Drucker has observed that the typical four-year college graduate is placed in a job that a normal 15-year-old could perform. A report to former Secretary of Health, Education, and Welfare Elliot L. Richardson stated, "Not only can work be redesigned to make it more satisfying, but significant increases in productivity can also be obtained—through job redesign." [7]

Job redesign involves analyzing the total content of the job and changing it to provide more interesting and challenging activity. As a result the job more fully utilizes the time, talent, and interest of the incumbent. Where the work activity itself proves more interesting and satisfying, there is greater motivation to exert effort, and thus productivity is increased.

Industrial democracy. In an article, "Sweden's Newest Export —Industrial Democracy," Derek Norcross stated, "Industrial democracy is an industrial revolution of sorts in which workers join with management in improving the quality of their work environment, the productivity of their labor, and the wealth of their nation." [8] In Sweden workers not only are represented in manage-

[7] Report of a Special Task Force to the Secretary of Health, Education, and Welfare (Cambridge, Mass.: The MIT Press, 1973), p. 94.
[8] *Parade Magazine,* December 15, 1974.

ment's major decision making but also are gaining a greater voice in how their jobs can be made more meaningful, interesting, and emotionally rewarding. Assembly lines are being redesigned to alleviate monotony, jobs are rotated in order to allow workers to broaden their skills, and workers are allowed to form teams to increase productivity and build a spirit of togetherness instead of alienation.

Pehr Gyllenhammer, president of Volvo, explained, "It's largely that our young people coming into the labor market will not take jobs which don't provide them with a sense of achievement and personal satisfaction. They are seeking some purpose to their labor beyond mere economic survival. Eventually American managers will have to face the same situation—that of a highly educated young labor force earnestly seeking job satisfaction." [9] An official of the Granges Company added, "Today, young people don't want a job they can learn in half an hour and just stand around moving their hands according to some fixed schedule. They want to know what it's all about. We've got to give them a chance to be aware of what they are doing and to influence their own situation." [10]

In the United States, General Motors and the United Auto Workers are cooperating in experiments along the same lines. Rockwell and others are also examining the contribution that the Swedish type of industrial democracy might make to job satisfaction, motivation, and productivity in this country.

Many managers will recognize that industrial democracy is one step beyond participative or interactive management. In participative management, individuals participate by making suggestions, discussing ideas, and interacting with management, but management retains the final decision and action to be taken. Industrial democracy goes the additional step of actually allowing workers to make the decisions and rearrange the physical and human work influences. It is an attempt to establish a sense of entrepreneurship into the highly automated and organized work environment that tends to dehumanize or belittle the whole personality and job needs of the individual. It seems likely that a younger, better-educated, more sophisticated and job-satisfaction-oriented employee popula-

[9] Ibid.
[10] Ibid.

tion will demand a voice in what influences their jobs as a condition for both their presence and effort. Various innovations in the newer area of industrial democracy provide an additional opportunity for companies to seek solutions to motivation and productivity.

Productivity modification. This involves both an overall and a detailed, in-depth analysis of all productivity influences and processes. Precisely what is being done, how is it being done, and what are the possibilities of improving results? Can the overall job performance be improved, and can the alteration of any one of the influences bring about better productivity?

Following is a list of the factors that researchers believe are important in influencing productivity. A comparison of these factors with current company practices reveals the productivity-related modifications that must be made in order to create the most favorable conditions for maximum production.

1. Employee compensation tied to performance and to sharing in productivity gains.
2. Participation of workers in decisions affecting their own and related jobs.
3. Job enlargement, including challenge, variety, wholeness, and self-regulation.
4. Employees' sense of involvement in the total organization.
5. Adequate safety conditions, pay, fringe benefits, and working conditions.
6. Simplification of channels of communication and authority.
7. Resources at workers' disposal to facilitate work effectiveness and reduce frustration associated with getting the job done.
8. Improved work methods that have involved workers in their planning and production.
9. Opportunities for greater employee "stewardship"; that is, direct care of and attention to customer/client/co-worker needs.
10. Allowance for flexibility in relation to type of incentive and authority patterns.

Serious efforts at productivity modification should elicit the continuing attention and response of both management and job incumbent. The individual doing the job repeatedly, but with an inquisitive will toward improvement, will discover shortcuts, time- and material-saving techniques, and ways of improving productivity. However, constructive productivity modification will be minimized unless it becomes a deliberate, systematic, and continuing activity that is both encouraged by and participated in by management and employee. Management's efforts and example should provide the pattern for demonstrating to and stimulating the individual to aggressively bring about productivity improvements. The amount of modification achieved depends on the input of management and its success in eliciting the enthusiastic participation of the employee. Management must show its interest in improvement, its serious appreciation of all employee input, and the benefit that the employee will receive through improved productivity.

Traditional forms of motivation, job enrichment, job redesign, and industrial democracy will not fill voids created by an ineffective physical and human organizational environment. But the motivational thrust can be reinforced by providing various forms of job enrichment that offers opportunities for making typical forms of leadership and job conditions even more effective.

HUMAN PRODUCTIVITY CHECKLIST

Productivity is the crux of the whole free enterprise system where supply and demand will establish prices and markets on a competitive basis. The physical environment, work arrangement, efficiency of equipment, and a variety of non-human factors influence productivity—both inside and outside the company. Companies can achieve a fairly even competitive level as far as the non-human factors are concerned. But human input remains the most crucial and flexible area in which productivity superiority must be achieved. It is the recognition of this reality that has caused companies to state, "Our people are our most important asset"; "the ideas and special skills of our people make the difference"; "you can't discount the special service our people give"; and "it is the quality of our people that makes the difference in the value of our product and service."

The following checklist can be used to analyze whether human contribution to productivity is being maximized:

1. In order to ascertain current productivity level (number of units produced and dollar sales per hour), compare results with similar companies.

2. Compare the cost to produce each unit or dollar of sales with similar companies.

3. Systematically analyze the efficiency of overall human productivity as provided for by the physical environment of the work area.

4. Measure the quality and availability of raw materials and other input needed for productivity to ensure that they do not impede performance.

5. Determine the overall competency of the individual to engage in both quantity and quality productive job activity.

6. Analyze motivational input by comparing productive output of individuals within the work group.

7. Analyze levels of risk versus degree of healthy challenge afforded by the job to determine whether it motivates the incumbent or impedes the individual's willingness to grow on the job.

8. Measure the influence of leadership on productivity as indicated by general morale and cooperation, employee turnover, ability and effort exerted, unit cost of production, and overall result on a departmental basis as compared with other departments.

9. Measure the ROI of human resources as a contribution to productivity or value added to company products and service.

During cyclical economic changes it is particularly critical to ensure that human productivity is at a profitable level. In a downturn, the survival of the company and individual jobs depends on keeping productive costs at an acceptable level. The many fixed expenses, over which only limited immediate action can be taken, force much of the burden of expense reduction on minimizing human cost. It is during changing and uncertain conditions that companies discover how efficient and productive their systems and people really are.

10
Providing
leadership
that achieves ROI

The amount of return on investment and the degree of utilization of human resources have a direct and decisive relationship to the quality of leadership at every level of the organization. It is supervisory leadership that makes the decisions affecting individual jobs, performance abilities, motivational commitment, attitudes, and permanence with the company. It is leadership that sets the personal example regarding a satisfactory relationship with the company and the job. It is leadership that organizes and assigns work and evaluates and rewards results. Leadership controls individual opportunity for job growth and satisfaction. In the final analysis, it is leadership that has the most penetrating influence on the overall cost of human resources as related to its contribution to the goals of the company.

A program to provide the most appropriate leadership should involve:

Identification of specific types of leadership required for maximum results.
Determination of the effectiveness of the present leadership.
A plan for providing the types of leadership needed.
The creation of a favorable human climate throughout the whole human resource group.

Guides for creating and maintaining leadership creditability.
Strengthening of the communication bridge between leadership
  and employee.
Constant monitoring and strengthening of leadership input.
Transition from individual to team strength.

In planning for appropriate leadership, it should be remembered
that the scope and influence of leadership have great impact on
every activity. The human framework in which the employee lives
on the job and performs his or her tasks is the byproduct of this
daily leadership. Few companies comprehend the full significance
of leadership influence on human contribution. Almost every survey, research project, and expert opinion indicates that leadership
has more influence on job performance than physical surround-
ings, human organization, or forms of compensation. The job-
related feeling, which precedes logic and decision making, is
directly influenced by what the leader demonstrates his or her feelings are concerning the employee. The employee needs to believe
that the supervisor is interested in him or her as an equal human
being and not just as an impersonal cog in the vast industrial production machine.

Companies that understand the decisive role of leadership in
the total scheme of activity will exert every possible effort to provide the type of leadership that will ensure desirable relationships
and human input. They recognize that it is leadership that makes
things happen and gets things done through people.

IDENTIFYING LEADERSHIP REQUIRED FOR RESULTS

One of management's most serious errors is its failure to
identify, understand, and define the appropriate types of leadership required to produce planned results. Leadership skills are often totally different from those required of effective engineers,
accountants, or salesmen, and it is impossible to provide appropriate leadership until there is a clear concept of what is required.
When promoted to department head, for example, the engineer,
who has spent a career concerned with mathematics, machines,
and precise measurements, must learn to manage and cope with a
whole new set of intangible human factors. When elected treasurer,

the accountant, who has been concerned with controls and utilization of financial resources, must adjust to the requirements of managing human resources. When promoted to sales manager, the salesperson must master a new set of skills because the success of this new job depends on the ability to manage other salespeople.

Psychologists, consultants, and experienced managers have their own lists of Boy Scout-type characteristics that a manager must possess to be an effective leader. The lists are often long and generally reflect the direct experience of the individual preparing the list. But before examining specific characteristics, it is important to consider the input that leadership should be expected to provide. This concept of leadership should include the following.

Impact on job-related behavior and performance. The most accurate measure of leadership is the degree of influence the leader has on the job-related activity of the individuals under his or her supervision. Effective leaders, coaches, generals, and managers exert a favorable influence on all human resources under their direction. Goal-achieving leadership must be able to bring about the type of effort and activity essential for job-related success. The sales manager must achieve sales goals through salespeople. The plant manager must turn out production through employees.

In order to bring about favorable influence on job behavior and cause appropriate activity to occur, the leader must provide certain input and create the type of climate that is most likely to accelerate this activity. It should be recognized that leadership, like motivation, has the capability of being either positive or negative. Certain motivational inputs can cause either more or less job effort. The key is to develop and provide that type of leadership that will result in maximum favorable impact on job behavior and performance. Human resource ROI is dependent on the type of leadership that will cause maximum favorable job influence to occur.

Performance results. The coach is judged by his team's record. The ship captain is rated according to the performance of his ship. The business and industrial leader should also be willing to be judged by the performance results of his or her unit. This is what the individual manager is being paid to do—produce results. He or she is not being paid to spend a certain number of hours on the job or to go through certain motions but to bring about a predetermined contribution.

Once input has been identified, concern must focus on results produced. What is the production result of individuals and the entire unit? How much do the salespeople sell and is the territory meeting its goal? ROI leadership is rated, compensated, and promoted according to results produced.

Identifiable tools and techniques. Leadership involves specific tools and techniques that must be skillfully used if expected results are to be produced. These would include communicating with employees, various forms of training and development, motivational techniques, individual correction and improvement of job performance, climate and attitude, human organization, and the various techniques available to the leader to achieve results through people. These involve the basic fundamentals of leadership and must be mastered and effectively implemented as a requirement for providing appropriate leadership.

Leadership activities. Certain essential activities must occur for leadership to function. These include assigning and reviewing work, solving problems, making decisions, and performing a variety of day-to-day services to employees. A test of leadership is to determine whether these activities are occurring and whether they are effective.

Special management skills. The company must respond to the premise that leadership consists of specific types of management skills that can be learned and improved. For example, managers can learn to be better communicators. The whole leadership system consists of identifiable processes, and just as a football player must learn and improve his skill in each fundamental of the game, so must the leader. Mastery of each process and activity becomes the fabric and glue of the complete leader.

Opportunity and obligation for change. Leadership should never be static; it should be dynamic and constantly in the process of change. The flow of change can be in the direction of less or more effectiveness. What change is the leader allowing or causing? What impact is the change having on job performance and results? ROI leadership functions as the catalytic element, causing those changes to occur that will lead to the achievement of desirable human and company goals.

CREATING A FAVORABLE HUMAN CLIMATE

Climate within the human organization is intangible and difficult to identify, but it has an influence on all human activity. It is basically the feeling and attitude people have about the company, their jobs, their supervisors, and their associates. It relates to the creditability of supervision, the overall effect of all job-related influences, and employees' perception of company policy. Climate indicates the predisposition to cooperate or dissent. Climate is the atmosphere, the mood, the gut feeling, the trust, the confidence, the degree of uptightness, and the understanding that exists in the work group.

The individual's immediate supervisor, regardless of level in the organization, has the greatest impact on climate. Just as a coach sets the tone, provides a sense of cohesiveness and teamwork, seeks a climate of mutual support and confidence, so should the supervisor. Company creeds, policies, work rules, job performance, reviews, opportunity for growth, and physical work environment also have an impact on climate.

An AMA survey, as reported in Table 6, reveals the influence of climate-related factors on productivity. Note the areas on which more than 75 percent of the respondents were in agreement.

Climate is often more feeling than fact. It is more a reflection of how an issue is perceived by people than the result of objective rationalization. The company might be able to prove by facts that the promotional policy is fair, but if Ed Smith has seniority in the accounting department and is bypassed for promotion, it might be difficult to convince him that the policy is fair. And as long as he remains unconvinced of the fairness of promotional practices, he sees the climate for his opportunity as one in which management plays favorites and promotes only those who cater to the boss.

The leader should be as concerned with climate as with job performance skills. It is from negative climate that many problems will stem—low morale, inadequate effort, lack of cooperation, complaints, and employee turnover. Significant favorable influences on climate can be achieved through:

Reasonable and understandable company policies.
Administering policies and relationships fairly.
Maintaining open lines of communication.

Ensuring complete understanding before, during, and after the fact regarding every decision.

Giving individuals reason to have confidence in and trust the supervisor, the company, and other members of the group.

The climate existing within a group can be monitored and measured in several ways: by analyzing overall results, by com-

Table 6. Opinions shared by more than 75% of group concerning the bearing of management-labor relations on productivity.

STATEMENT	PERCENT AGREEING	PERCENT DISAGREEING
1. To produce more with the same amount of human effort is a sound economic and social objective.	96	3
2. It is possible for the union and management to cooperate on specific programs that will improve productivity.	92	6
3. Improving the quality of work life is a desirable management goal even if it doesn't increase productivity.	89	10
4. Relations between workers and management would improve if the benefits of productivity improvement were shared with workers.	75	21
5. The interests of management and workers are, by and large, in conflict.	21	77
6. Few managers and supervisors are genuinely concerned about workers and their jobs.	22	77
7. Since jobs are scarce, a greater emphasis on productivity may jeopardize jobs.	14	85
8. The "human relations" approach is a device for undermining the union.	8	89

Source: Mildred E. Katzell, *Productivity: The Measure and the Myth,* AMACOM, 1975.

paring the number and type of complaints from the group, and by
checking employee turnover rate and reasons for turnover. The
quality of product and service produced by members of the group
can be analyzed. Employees' attitude and morale, and the degree
to which individuals have confidence in leadership and company,
can be ascertained. In addition, accidents, customer complaints,
and other indicators of employee attitude and job commitment can
be analyzed.

Many techniques are available for determining the quality of
the human climate within a department or company. Perhaps the
most effective is face-to-face relationship with individuals in which
management is willing to listen, really hear, and become accurately
aware of how individuals perceive and feel about the climate in
which they work. Another commonly used technique is the morale
survey, attitude survey, or job information survey, which can be
conducted by outside consultants or internally by the company. It
can consist of forms completed by employees or personal interviews. If properly used, it can be an effective tool for determining
and improving climate. However, this type of instrument should
not be treated as a "plaything" by management; it should be managed as carefully as the financial side of the business. In order to
result in constructive change, a survey should include the following:

—A professionally designed form or interview that is carefully constructed to achieve its goal.
—A thorough and accurate explanation to employees regarding the purpose and procedure involved.
—Anonymity to the extent that the employee believes that
what is revealed will not adversely affect his or her relationship with the supervisor or associates or any aspect regarding
his or her job.
—Tangible and overt evidence on the part of management that
it is responding to and doing something about situations and
problems revealed by the survey.

The job information survey enables the employee to make
important personal and job information available to the company.
The company in turn has the opportunity of using the information
to make improvements.

The job information survey shown in Figure 9 provides an audit of what employees believe about the company, its policies, leadership, pay, benefits, opportunity, and ways in which the company can be improved. The survey is inexpensive to conduct and makes available data that can be useful in making constructive changes, preparing training programs, building teamwork, and demonstrating management's concern for employee input.

It should be assumed that employees know their legal and company-provided job rights. They also develop an understanding regarding whether these entitlements are being administered fairly and to their best interests. This knowledge, along with changing lifestyles, provides both the boldness and willingness for employees to complain to management and outside agencies if they feel they are treated unfairly.

In the interest of giving the company the best return on investment, appropriate attention and time must be allocated to constructing and maintaining a favorable human climate. It has a decisive impact on both quantity and quality of production, relationships within the group, and individual permanence on the job. Climate becomes the invisible spirit of the group that tilts attitudes, efforts, and feelings toward a positive or negative direction. It is a decisive ingredient that management and individual leadership are responsible for initiating, directing, and maintaining.

BUILDING THE COMMUNICATIONS BRIDGE

Leaders and subordinates who have not reached mutual understanding are disjointed and function as isolated pieces that fail to serve their own best interests or those of the company. The leader has goals to achieve, as well as an understanding of how to accomplish them. The subordinate also understands the goals involved and has personal needs that he or she hopes will be met through the job. The goals and aspirations of leader and subordinate should be mutual and should be accurately linked if each is to achieve expectations. This ideal condition results from constant, creditable, and accurate communication by both parties. There is a need to identify these goals and aspirations and to use them as a basis for communication between leaders and subordinates at every level. Whether this need is met depends on management's willing-

Figure 9. *Job information survey.*

Name and Location _____

Hours normally worked per week _____

Check One: Supervisor _____ Salesperson _____ Sales Supporting _____

Code: U=unsatisfactory, F=fair, S=satisfactory, G=good, E=excellent

AREAS OF JOB INTEREST	Check the one that most nearly applies				
	U	F	S	G	E
1. My company's reputation in the community is	( )	( )	( )	( )	( )
2. If a friend asked me about getting a job here, I'd say this place is	( )	( )	( )	( )	( )
3. My company's customer service reputation is	( )	( )	( )	( )	( )
4. My company's merchandise reputation is	( )	( )	( )	( )	( )
5. The general working conditions, rest rooms and physical facilities are	( )	( )	( )	( )	( )
6. Management's promptness in making corrections and changes that are needed is	( )	( )	( )	( )	( )
7. The fairness of the company personnel policies and procedures is	( )	( )	( )	( )	( )
8. The fairness of customer-related company policies and procedures is	( )	( )	( )	( )	( )
9. Management's concern for employees as individuals is	( )	( )	( )	( )	( )
10. The courtesy and helpfulness received when using my employee discount are	( )	( )	( )	( )	( )
11. My knowledge of employee benefits is	( )	( )	( )	( )	( )
12. Our total employee benefits (vacation, discounts, profit sharing, etc.) as compared to other retailers are	( )	( )	( )	( )	( )
13. The extent to which I understand the basis of my rate of pay is	( )	( )	( )	( )	( )
14. The extent to which training enables me to do a better job and increase my pay is	( )	( )	( )	( )	( )
15. The amount of initial training I received was	( )	( )	( )	( )	( )
16. The extent to which I feel "tuned in" to what's happening throughout the store is	( )	( )	( )	( )	( )
17. The extent to which I am informed ahead of time regarding changes that affect my work is	( )	( )	( )	( )	( )
18. My understanding of duties and responsibilities is	( )	( )	( )	( )	( )
19. My understanding of how well I am expected to do my job (amount of sales, etc.) is	( )	( )	( )	( )	( )

AREAS OF JOB INTEREST	Check the one that most nearly applies				
	U	F	S	G	E
20. The extent to which I have the opportunity to develop and use my full potential on my job is	( )	( )	( )	( )	( )
21. When I do a job well, the recognition I receive is	( )	( )	( )	( )	( )
22. My opportunities for a fair and reasonable chance for promotion and increased pay are	( )	( )	( )	( )	( )
23. Cooperation among employees in my department and throughout the company is	( )	( )	( )	( )	( )
24. The respect and confidence I have in my supervisor are	( )	( )	( )	( )	( )
25. When talking to my supervisor, the freedom I feel in saying what is on my mind is	( )	( )	( )	( )	( )
26. My supervisor's willingness to listen and assist me when I have questions, problems, etc. is	( )	( )	( )	( )	( )
27. My supervisor's encouragement of me to offer suggestions and to try better ways to do things is	( )	( )	( )	( )	( )

28. Which employee benefit(s) are most valuable to you? _____
    _____
    Why? _____

29. In my opinion, the main problem that stands in our way for increased sales is
    _____
    _____

30. Do you have a job performance review with your supervisor at least once a year? Yes _____ No _____

31. Do you have training meetings? _____ How often? _____
    By whom conducted? _____

32. What type of additional training would you like to have? _____
    _____

33. What do you like most about working here? _____
    _____

34. What do you like least about working here? _____
    _____

35. What would your recommendations be to improve this company as a place to work? _____
    As a place to shop? _____
    _____

ness and initiative in allowing employees to know, to participate, to understand, and to contribute.

Communication has been discussed, written about, trained around, and chosen by management as the theme for conventions perhaps more than any other subject. And still it is the one that has achieved the least progress or result. Today our business environment is one of computers, visual aids, duplicating machines, audio and visual novelties, canned programs, electronic linkups, and an endless variety of communications tools. But in the final analysis, communication is most importantly a one-to-one relationship rather than a formal or programmed process. What is the relationship of the individuals who need to communicate with each other? Does the receiver trust and have confidence in the sender? Is the why, or purpose, of communication explained and understood?

The premise of ROI depends on productivity, which in turn depends on adequate understanding. The catalog of ROI ingredients relies on the linkage of communications from top to bottom and back up. In testing the effectiveness of the communications, the following should be considered.

1. Is there evidence that individuals understand what the company expects of them and what they can expect of the company? Lack of communication in this area results in inadequate understanding—leading to negative employee relations, disappointment on the part of both company and employee, and lessened job effort.

2. Is there evidence that the requirements of the job are understood and accepted? Most jobs involve certain work rules, safety guides, time requirements, and factors regarding how the job should be done. Job activity by individuals should demonstrate that there is adequate understanding and acceptance. Often, unsatisfactory performance is the result of inadequate information or acceptance of the reasons for the requirements.

3. Do production results demonstrate that the incumbent understands and accepts the performance goals established? Although initial and continuing training should establish required knowledge, skills and effort, the day-to-day communication between supervisor and employee has a much stronger and more permanent impact on production results.

4. Do activities and trends in each unit of management demonstrate that communication is being used to move all forces in a favorable and constructive direction? What is the trend of employee grievances, absenteeism, and turnover? A strong influence on the direction these forces take is the quality of communication throughout the company, especially at the superior–subordinate point of contact.

What contribution should communication make to ROI in human resources? Is it being achieved? Leadership must inform, clarify, persuade, and move in a productive, goal-oriented direction. Force, coercion, threats, and rewards have proved inadequate. Creating the environment through communication in which productivity activity will occur is the most effective avenue available to company leadership. Deliberate, continuous, and effective effort should be applied to ensure that appropriate communication is occurring, since it is the bridge over which productivity activity must move.

MONITORING SUPERVISORY LEADERSHIP

How really effective is the supervisory leadership throughout the organization? Since leadership is a vital ingredient for profitable productivity, its effectiveness should be constantly monitored, refined, and improved. The ROI of the company's expenditure for the time, presence, and talents of supervisors is based on the contribution made by these leaders to the goals of the organization. This contribution must be made largely through the supervisors' influence on the job performance of others.

Monitoring superivsory leadership involves the following key checkpoints.

Competency and performance of subordinates. The supervisor of every department must possess the qualifications to see that the work is properly carried out in his or her area; this responsibility cannot be passed to a training department or other area of the company. It can be supplemented by others, and the supervisor can seek competent guidance, but in the end the monkey comes to rest on his or her back. Monitoring leadership contribution, therefore, involves measuring the competency and performance of the subordinates of each supervisor.

Organizational framework of leadership. Periodic reviews should be made regarding the written versus the functioning position description, delegated authority, standards of performance, and goals for each supervisor. Too often, what higher management agreed to and placed in a dusty, undisturbed file is not what the supervisor currently understands regarding the framework and requirements of the position. Monitoring leadership means constantly reviewing, refining, updating, and making more realistic the operating framework of every leadership position. This determines whether the framework is appropriate and whether it is providing a positive thrust toward goals assigned to the position.

Indicators of climate, attitude, and response to leadership. The greatest single influence on optional absenteeism and employee turnover is the quality of supervision. The number and severity of grievances generally relate to attitudes and creditability of leadership. The acceptance and achievement of production goals fairly accurately reflect leadership effectiveness. Compliance with safety rules, work policies, employee benefit guides, quality standards, and other company requirements is a measure of leadership performance.

Comparison with other in-company units and outside operations. In most companies, physical working conditions, pay and employee benefit structure, and company-provided job influences are similar throughout. The biggest difference existing between areas is leadership. Significant variance in human climate and performance results can be attributed to the difference in leadership. When the variance exists in a negative direction, it indicates that the quality of leadership should be improved. Also, if the cost of producing a product or service is greater than it is in similar companies, the contribution of leadership should be suspect.

Even though quality people have been employed, it is extremely important that companies not assume that training and development is occurring, that the organizational framework is professional, that all elements are aimed in a goal-oriented direction, and that ultimate achievement will occur. Effective means of monitoring leadership effectiveness should be structured into the total operational process.

CREATING AND MAINTAINING
LEADERSHIP CREDITABILITY

How much trust can be placed in the boss? Can subordinates count on what he or she says and promises? Creditability influences attitude, effort, and performance. A psychologist was asked to suggest a test to determine whether employees felt that their supervisor was trustworthy. He recommended that employees ask themselves, "In the event of your death, and in the absence of a will, would you trust your supervisor to administer your estate in a completely honest manner most beneficial to your spouse and family?"

Whether an individual feels comfortable and secure hinges largely on whether he or she can trust and depend on members of the group—especially the leader, who has the greatest influence on the thinking and action of the group. Before inhibition and holdbacks are abandoned in favor of unrestrained effort, subordinates must have confidence in their supervisor.

Supervisors are prone to agree on the importance of creditability, but are mystified as to what it consists of and how it can be created and maintained. The characteristics listed here are the building blocks of creditability. A creditable leader is one who:

Clarifies what is expected and encourages its achievement by engaging in the activity.

Gives access to information needed and establishes work guides, but permits freedom regarding how results will be achieved.

Doesn't oversupervise, ask too many questions, or interfere as long as the job is being done in a satisfactory manner.

Is tough enough to insist on results but permits others to be honest and staunch in their positions.

Is consistent, does not change his or her mind too often.

Insists that others be consistent by seeing that policies and rules are followed fairly and uniformly.

Proves dependability by being available, keeping promises, and being willing to explain why.

Is willing to fight the battles for the employee, when merited, regarding working conditions, pay, benefits, and promotions.

Listens carefully and purposely and responds to the limits of his or her capability.

Is a friendly human being with empathy and understanding rather than a boss devoid of reasonable compassion.

Builds through every contact and activity a track record of trustworthiness and creditability.

Creditability building might have to start from a neutral or even negative position. It might involve a slow, tedious, uphill struggle. But it should always involve a conscious, deliberate, and systematic effort on the part of the supervisor. Most importantly, it must be sincere, real, and felt; play-acting facades will be detected quickly and rejected by employees.

In our modern age of mistrust of bigness, government, business, educators, products, services, guarantees, fine print, and a quicksand environment, employees transfer this skepticism to company leadership—all the way from immediate supervisor to president. Yet it should be recognized that what the company achieves is directly related to its creditability with its entire workforce. Creditability deserves a high priority of management's time and support if acceptable ROI in human resources is to be achieved.

FROM INDIVIDUAL POTENTIAL
TO TEAM STRENGTH

The athletic coach and the business leader face similar challenges in taking individuals with potential and molding them into a cohesive performing force that achieves competitive superiority in the form of a winning score or a superior product. Although most management attention is focused on the competency and performance of the individual, it is the interactive result of team performance that can be decisive. The transformation of individual potential into a result-producing force greater than the sum of the individual members is the challenge of team building in every work unit.

The coach studies the competition and the available talent and then attempts to devise a winning plan of action. He or she engages in strategy sessions with his associates, makes certain that members of the team know and understand the nature of their competition, uses skull sessions and illustrations to clarify the game plan and individual responsibility for implementing the plan, has pep talks before the game, and makes strategy and tactical moves during the game.

Few business leaders take a similar approach to team building within the work group. However, utilization of the full talent potential of individuals depends on effective social and task interaction with the leader and other members of the team. Although an often neglected and little understood leadership responsibility, effective team building can make a significant contribution to job performance. Rensis Likert stated the case for team building:

> Management will make full use of the potential capabilities of its human resources only when each person in an organization is a member of one or more effectively functioning work groups that have a high degree of group loyalty, effective skills of interaction and high performance goals.[1]

In addition to the company's concern for teamwork, the employee has certain needs that are best served through the work group by linking individual goals with those of the group for increased personal achievement and success, and by providing certain company-related personal expectations that can be achieved through social contact and daily interaction with other members of the group. Individuals thus satisfy the innate need to share their activities, achievements, and even their sorrows with others. The eight-hour, five-day week affords the largest amount of human interaction available. People also need to feel important and to know they are needed by others. The group provides a sense of identity for the employee and allows him or her to feel he or she is vital to the group by making a meaningful contribution.

Performing and contributing as a member of the team are more challenging and rewarding than they are on an individual basis. Shooting baskets alone can become boring but becomes exciting and rewarding when one is a member of a winning basketball team. A work task can be boring and unrewarding when devoid of team contact, but it becomes both challenging and rewarding when performed while interacting as a member of a work team. The need of the individual for team identification, participation, recognition,

[1] Rensis Likert, *New Patterns of Management* (New York: McGraw-Hill Book Company, Inc., 1961), p. 99.

and reward provides the leader with a ready-made opportunity for team building for the benefit of both employee and company.

GUIDES FOR TEAM BUILDING

Team success depends on maximum utilization of the potential of every individual. Full individual participation and reward are essential ingredients. Teamwork can achieve results that are not attainable through individual effort. The movement from individual potential to team strength involves the following prerequisites.

Understanding of and commitment to group goals by individual members. Commitment depends on each individual's knowing and accepting the reasons for effort and team contribution. The individual needs to perceive the impact of his or her contribution on team performance and the role that the group result has on the team or total company. It is desirable that this comprehension be communicated on both a short- and long-range basis—short-range feedback serving as reinforcement for future contribution.

Opportunity for meaningful participation. The coach or leader should deliberately and systematically solicit the participation of every individual in goal-oriented decision making. When the coach calls the quarterback to the sidelines, he asks what play will move the football toward the goal. The supervisor asks, "What are your ideas? How do you think we can best solve this problem?" The guiding principle is that individuals will commit more quickly and more fully to activities and requirements that they feel they have had a hand in initiating and designing. Not only are participation and shared leadership effective team builders, but also, in most instances, they produce superior results. And just as an effective coach refuses to accept non-involvement, but draws in and insists on participation by every member of the group, so must the supervisor. This ensures that every member of the team will experience and benefit from having been involved. Some individuals need to be encouraged, coached, gently pushed, and challenged in order to bring them into full contribution.

Individual flexibility. All individuals are different. They vary in their needs and in their reactions at different times. The team builder recognizes the differential of team members and uses this flexibility to strengthen the team. He or she is sensitive to the needs of each individual and enables each to achieve his or her needs in relation to his or her contribution to team goals. The leader brings together—meshing and linking, very carefully and deliberately—the individuality and unique perceptions of each employee. Each employee thus serves to strengthen all other members of the team and multiply the results achieved.

Maximum utilization of individual talents, competencies, and potential. The successful team builder recognizes individual skills and potential and finds ways for each employee to make a full contribution. The coach builds the team and strategy on the basis of the strength and weakness of each player. The supervisor follows the same procedure in building a team. Individuals bring to the team various experiences, backgrounds, education, interests, hobbies, skills, aspirations, needs, preferences, and levels of responsiveness. The team's strength and effectiveness depend on the full utilization of these resources.

Openness and freedom to communicate and interact. Ideally, members of the team must trust one another. They must want to see other members achieve and succeed. They should feel comfortable discussing job-related (and sometimes non-job) problems and ideas. They should experience a sense of pride in the group and what it stands for. They should be tolerant of individual differences of lifestyles, opinions, and philosophies without letting them minimize team cohesion and effectiveness. The self-interest of the team is served through friendly, trusting, open, and continuous interaction by all its members.

Too many individuals assume they can isolate themselves from others, work hard in their own areas of responsibility, and produce successful results. It will never happen. In corporate enterprise, success depends on an effective two-way, interacting relationship with others. The four key influences on achievement are the boss, peers, subordinates, and the public (often customers). Personal contribution is vital, but maximum result depends on the members of the team.

Team development of procedures and solutions for dealing with challenges and problems. There will be specific problems, emergencies, changes, and major challenges where acceptable solutions will hinge on the group's innovation and creativity. Although decisions based on a consensus of opinion are not always the surest solution to a winning athletic or industrial score, the group-initiated solution should be encouraged and given full consideration. Often major changes, which must have the full cooperation of everyone, will fail unless understanding and acceptance of the changes have been achieved through joint development.

Willingness to work within the team framework and follow guidelines. The members of the team should agree mutually on the responsibility and role of each participant—not everyone can play quarterback or be the supervisor. The problems and goals should be fully understood. Once plans have been finalized, employees should give full commitment. Each should be willing to work within reasonable guidelines toward the goals selected. Major functions involve logical and sequential steps best suited to their successful completion. Individuals must be willing to follow these steps and work in harmony with others in abiding by all work-related guides set forth for the team.

An experience of personal success through membership on a winning team. Employees should recognize that their individual goals will seldom be achieved in an unsuccessful department or company. The motivation for team cooperation, effort, and contribution should be individual self-interest. There are few individual winners on losing teams. Professional recruiters look to winning teams for their future stars. Promotions, pay increases, and recognition are more likely to occur when the department is successful. The key to the individual's commitment to the team will therefore depend on his or her concept of how his or her personal aspirations can be achieved through the contribution he or she makes to the team.

Creating team strength. The weak links in the team chain must be found. Does the group consist of 11 individuals headed in an equal number of different directions or a team composed of 11 members fully integrated and committed to a single set of goals? It is the leader's responsibility to coordinate and direct each person's potential, goals, and contributions into a well-functioning, winning team. This requires the highest form of human skills in training, motivation, human psychology, professional management, and common sense. It requires being friendly and human, being responsive to individual feelings and needs, firmness in requiring disciplined effort, and continuing attention to refining and improving the effectiveness of the team.

Appropriate company framework and leadership can lead individuals into productive group job performance. Groups need not develop in a helter-skelter fashion, but can be directed into mature, constructive channels. Group effectiveness depends on appropriate leadership, which in turn develops team cooperation and contribution. The leader, in conjunction with employees, is responsible for eliminating internal conflict, promoting harmony, linking and integrating energies, and moving from individual potential to full team achievement.

Acceptable ROI will not be achieved in human resources if the vital ingredient of appropriate leadership is missing. Team cohesion, strength, commitment, and the foundation of company success become the result of leadership at all levels. Leadership should be expected to make specific contributions which can be identified, measured, monitored, and improved. The goal interests of everyone concerned will best be served through management's effectiveness in ensuring that appropriate leadership is provided through the company.

11

Retaining, compensating, and utilizing human resources

At various management conventions and seminars, I have posed this question: "Suppose when you return to your company tomorrow you learn that the top 25 percent of your best producers, sellers, and various levels of management have resigned. What would your reaction be?" The look on most faces is first one of puzzlement and then of impending doom. The answers have ranged from "I'd shoot myself" to "The company wouldn't survive." Yet rather strangely, most managers and companies admit that they don't have, and have never really given much attention to, an identifiable program for retaining that 25 percent or the other 75 percent of the human resources essential to survival and growth.

One of the main responsibilities of the financial executive is the preservation of capital. Every manager responsible for plants, equipment, and machinery is concerned with maintenance and continuing, trouble-free operation. Although programs for conserving capital and physical assets are systematic, deliberate, and well planned, similar programs are relatively non-existent for the protection and preservation of human resources. But if human resources were lost, this asset would be the most difficult to replace, would take longer to bring to acceptable levels of productivity, and would cause the greatest interference with the achievement of company goals.

An acceptable ROI in human resources requires adequate attention and programs for protecting and preserving the human asset that has been created. Protecting ROI is concerned with programs that ensure retention through compensation, other forms of job satisfaction, and full utilization. A review of the amount of the organization's investment in human resources and the company's dependence on this asset should stimulate a deliberate program for its preservation.

RETAINING THE HUMAN ASSET

Retention depends on the individual's understanding and believing that the advantages of staying are greater than the advantages of leaving. This fact of corporate life leads to an examination of what employees want from their jobs and what provides job satisfaction. It also calls attention to those areas that cause dissatisfaction and therefore that might lead to resignation. It is concerned with human conditions within the company and how well these influences (pay, benefits, and working conditions) compare with similarly skilled positions in other companies. The goal is a favorable human environment that is able to compete with the advantages offered by other companies. The degree to which management allows this climate to deteriorate will determine the number of valuable employees lost—often the highly skilled, promotable ones most essential to company success.

Many separations are the result of single incidents or goofs on the part of supervisors. It is doubtful that many employees are totally pleased with their job-related conditions, but unless a catalyst is provided, only a few will take the initiative to resign. This often comes in the form of a supervisor who criticizes unfairly or in an embarrassing manner, promotes employees without explanation to those not promoted, or fails to live up to promises. The employee concludes, "I think my opportunities and job satisfaction might be greater elsewhere. At least it's worth taking a chance, since it appears that I won't be treated fairly or have a chance to get ahead here."

A general analysis of key areas influencing job permanence should include these matters:

The levels and types of compensation and benefits.

The availability of training and development opportunities.

An accurate assessment of the concepts held by employees of the value the company placed on them as individuals and how well the company really treats them.

The quality of leadership and relationship between supervised and supervisor.

The physical working conditions—whether positive or negative.

The degree to which talents and potential are fully utilized through the promotion and transfer system.

The types and amount of information the employee receives and finds credible through the company's various forms of communication.

The degree of understanding the employee has regarding his or her job, results expected, and the manner in which job performance will be judged and rewarded.

The employee's trust in the company and its leaders.

The influence tilting the scales for staying or leaving is seldom only one of the above items; it is usually a mix of several. Therefore, the company program for retention must contain a blend of benefits and job environment that will be given a favorable overall rating by the employee.

BALANCED, COMPETITIVE, AND INCENTIVE COMPENSATION

Employees work for money. They will often work harder for more money. They will leave if pay is not satisfactory. But employees should never be paid in money alone—they also need other forms of psychic income or job satisfaction.

Although employees insist on other forms of compensation in addition to money, it is pay that becomes one of the keys for attracting, motivating, and retaining people. There are many factors influencing value placed on pay by the individual:

Actual need. This will be influenced by lifestyle, age, size of family, payments to be met, and employee's effectiveness in managing money.

Educational attainment. Individuals who have invested more time and money in obtaining more education expect higher and quicker pay results.

Expectation based on personal environment. This involves earning levels of parents, relatives, friends, and peers.

What the individual believes to be a fair rate for the job level. This is based on what the employee believes about the duties, responsibilities, and contribution of the job.

Current earnings. Whether this is acceptable would be influenced by length of employment, time in present job, and time elapsed since last increase.

Amount of pay as related to pay of others. This involves the extent to which the individual perceives the fairness of pay in relationship to the pay of other employees in similar jobs.

Concepts the individual has regarding how and what must occur in order to earn more money. This involves the extent to which the individual understands what must take place, what must be done differently, how much production or sales must increase, what job performance rating must be attained, and the impact of these on the amount of compensation. The individual should be able to understand beforehand and then experience afterward a predictable relationship between job contribution and pay.

In constructing, altering, and administering a compensation program, the company should establish specific goals. Compensation, properly administered, should become a key ingredient for enabling the company to achieve its financial goals. Robert E. Sibson suggests that such a goal-oriented compensation program should meet the following objectives:

1. It should be structured so as to help attract and retain the numbers and kinds of employees required to operate the business. . . .
2. The program should help to maintain the company in a reasonably competitive position in its product market. . . .
3. The nature of the program and the associated administrative costs must be reasonable and must be in proportion to the other priorities and time demands on the company's financial resources and available management time.
4. The program must gain employee acceptance. . . .
5. The compensation program must play a positive role in motivat-

ing employees to perform their duties to the best of their abilities and in a manner which supports the achievement of enterprise goals.

6. The program must gain acceptance by the firm's "public"— which includes owners; government; and, to some extent, customers, investors, and general public.

7. The compensation program must provide opportunity for employees at every level to achieve their reasonable aspirations in a framework of equity, impartiality, and reasonableness.[1]

COMPENSATION REQUIREMENTS

Since compensation represents one of the largest single operating costs for many companies, ROI is dependent on a predictable and controlled expense that in turn produces an appropriate contribution. In order for this to occur, a compensation plan should be properly constructed in these ways:

It should be a formal plan, and in writing.

It should provide for advance budgeting that will keep the payroll costs at an acceptable level.

It should maintain an appropriate balance between fixed pay, incentives, and bonuses. This means that a percentage of total compensation should be guaranteed and paid on a regular basis. In addition, incentives—based on performance and contribution—should be available, where practical.

It must be communicated in understandable form to employees. They should understand the basis of their pay and how they can earn more. In many job information surveys in which I have been involved, lack of understanding of the method of pay and how more could be earned has been the number one complaint of employees.

Pay rates should be based on job evaluation, and increases in pay should be based on performance.

It should enable managers to solve their daily pay problems and get the answers employees need regarding compensation (many problems are outside the authority of the immediate supervisor).

It should provide adequate records and a systematic, scheduled

[1] Robert E. Sibson, *Compensation,* AMACOM, 1974.

review of performance to determine whether increases are merited.

It should provide for continuing increases and should stimulate career growth.

It must be a plan that individuals accept as being reasonably fair, and it should provide equitable compensation for the work performed in relation to the overall benefit derived by the company.

It must meet all legal requirements regarding various aspects of compensation.

Most individuals have a reasonable idea of what their work ought to be worth to the company. False or grandiose notions about pay are often the result of incorrect or inadequate information.

Excessive compensation costs and negative employee relations problems are generally the result of an improperly constructed, communicated, or administered compensation program. Pay that is tied to properly evaluated duties and responsibilities, job contribution, and levels of decision making should enable the company to solve its human relations goals of attracting, retaining, and obtaining maximum job effort.

A properly managed compensation plan can be of great assistance to the company in attracting, motivating, retaining, and rewarding a fully qualified and effective workforce. Appropriate compensation administration assures management that payroll dollars will be spent in the most effective manner. Employees should know that their pay will be commensurate with their contribution. Compensation planning deserves the most careful and continuing attention of top management and technically qualified staff specialists. Management incurs considerable risk to the whole concept of ROI in human resources if compensation matters are neglected. In budgeting and changing compensation structures, the important impact on employee benefits should be considered. Pay levels for Social Security, vacations, holidays, sick leave, profit sharing, and other types of pay for time not worked are tied to the compensation rate. Many companies have experienced sizable financial shock after computing increased benefit costs imposed by changes in pay rates.

FUTURE COMPENSATION CONSIDERATIONS

Compensation experts are giving increased attention to total compensation and allowing individual differences to influence types of compensation. More planning will be focused on:

The creative, fast-track person.

Supplemental compensation in the form of health-maintenance facilities and delayed pay in the form of stock options.

Material rewards versus status symbols as motivators.

Relationship of rewards to objectives achieved.

Meshing of individual and group goals.

Relationship of compensation to company profit and growth.

Flexibility of amount of time worked.

Straight salary and guaranteed income for hourly employees.

Pay in lieu of benefits.

Overtime pay for managers and professionals.

A variety of compensation choices.

Flexible compensation also means changing forms of compensation according to age—for example, emphasizing pay and life insurance while children are at home but shifting to security and retirement when the children are on their own.

THE COST AND VALUE OF BENEFITS

Although compensation has increased rapidly since World War II, the cost of employee benefits has increased even faster. Some benefits, such as Social Security, are legally required and the company has no control over these rates of increase. In other areas, the pressure comes from competition, genuine employee needs, and changing patterns of expectations. To the direct payroll cost, as revealed by a U.S. Chamber of Commerce Survey, must be added $1.54 per hour, or $3,230 per year, as the cost for employee benefits or fringe wages. The amount spent for benefits ranks third behind payroll and purchasing as a percent of total operating costs. It must be included along with direct wages as part of the cost of human time. The reasons for providing various forms of "pay for time not worked" is basically the same as for providing direct payroll—to attract, motivate, and retain a high-quality workforce. Unfortunately, employees seldom give the company credit for the expenses incurred in providing these fringe benefits.

Once granted, employee benefits—like a pay increase—are very difficult to lower or take away. Benefits is an area in which extreme caution must be exercised with regard to designing and administering various plans. The immediate as well as long-range impact should be calculated. For example, life insurance, pensions, and various forms of benefits increase with length of service and at retirement become built-in future costs. If the company is sizable and in-house expertise is not available, actuaries and consultants are often needed.

The most common error in benefit planning is the piecemeal approach whereby each benefit is added or increased without regard to its impact on the total benefit cost. Pressures are created because a competitor is granting an additional holiday, an extra week of vacation, or more medical insurance coverage. In order to be competitive, management increases the benefit without taking into consideration the fact that the company might be superior to competitors in many other areas and is already spending a greater percentage of payroll for benefits.

The sensible benefit-planning approach is to provide a total package. Benefits should be analyzed, increased, and communicated as a total program of benefits. A comparison of the total is the most meaningful measure of whether the company is truly competitive. Focus on the total benefit package prevents employee downgrading of individual benefits because some other company might be superior in just one benefit.

Utilization of employee benefits as a positive, goal-oriented contribution toward ensuring ROI means that eight steps must be followed on a continuing basis:

1. Compute accurately current and future costs of all benefits.

2. Control and administer all costs of benefits as carefully as expenditures for any other purpose.

3. Stress the value of the total benefit package and be able to translate these benefits into additional compensation dollars received. Many companies annually give each employee a printed statement indicating the amount of his or her pay during the previous year, along with a detailed explanation of what was provided for the employee and family by way of benefits.

4. Use as many types of communication (meetings, individual explanations, printed media, and so on) as necessary to make certain that employees understand fully all details of employee benefits. The company gets very little credit for its expenditure if the employee is unaware of benefits or does not understand how they work.

5. When making individual decisions about employment, separations, transfers, revised work schedules, and pay changes, consider the cost impact on employee benefits. Many benefits are based on length of service and number of hours worked and therefore might be a consideration in making changes that might affect the total benefit cost of a unit.

6. Audit records to ensure that only eligible employees are granted benefits. The company should be just as conscientious about not spending money for benefits to ineligible employees as it is about making certain that each employee receives every benefit to which the policy entitles him or her.

7. Make certain that all benefits are made available and administered in compliance with legal requirements and in a nondiscriminatory manner.

8. Remind employees that benefits are provided by the company and function as fringe wages to which they are entitled as a part of their compensation.

Employee benefits are intended as a motivator, but they can become negative if they are not properly designed, balanced, administered, and communicated. Although the company has to work both smart and hard to get credit for the benefits it sustains, it has little choice of whether benefits are provided. If the company wants to be considered progressive and a good place to work, it must provide competitive benefits. It might not get full credit for providing benefits, but it will get full blame and negative consequences if benefits are not provided. Properly designing and administering employee benefits is the company's only real option for ensuring ROI from benefit costs. Employee benefit programs, like a stock portfolio, should be constantly evaluated for both adequacy of design and cost control. Substantial benefits can also be provided to employees at a minimum of cost through assistance with personal problems through budgetary guides, referrals for counseling, and answers to job-related concerns.

ENSURING FULL UTILIZATION OF TALENT

What is the dollar value of time and talent wasted each year by the company? How many employees are in jobs that do not make maximum use of the time and potential being purchased? How many jobs are not making their planned contribution because they are filled by employees performing below expectations? These questions should stimulate the development of programs to cope with the challenge of making full use of the time and talent available for the benefit of the company and the individual. From the ROI standpoint, the company cannot afford to waste the time and talent assets it has purchased. From the individual perspective, failure to find opportunities for full use of time and abilities leads to dissatisfaction and eventual resignation. When this occurs, the company has failed to protect its asset.

A useful tool for ensuring full utilization of talent is the employee activity profile shown in Figure 10. The profile provides information for management decision making, assures employees that all essential information regarding their work records is known to management, and facilitates compliance with government regulations. Making the maximum use of talent and potential involves:

—Achieving the best match-up of jobs and employees on the basis of skills, knowledge, and job requirements.

—Making use of a skills catalog or file that shows the qualifications of all individuals. Possibly many of these skills are not being used in the current job assignment.

—Providing for appropriate evaluation of performance and potential to make certain that abilities and potential are not overlooked.

—Designing and administering career planning programs to ensure that individuals are aware of future opportunities and that they have a realistic approach to achieving them.

—Reviewing and, where appropriate, recycling individuals through additional training, different jobs, or new career paths.

—Making certain that individuals are freed for training, promotions, and advantageous transfers.

—Creating a climate in which managers and employees have ready access to discuss promotions and career-related information. It is in this area that the supervisor can render a very real service

Figure 10. Employee activity profile.

NAME _____

DATE OF EMPLOYMENT _____

FIRST POSITION WITH XYZ COMPANY _____

FIRST LOCATION _____

Training and Development Record*

Date Offered	Course (List any course offered while with XYZ Company)	Employee accepted/ rejected	Date Enrolled	Date Completed	Tuition paid by company	Comments

Performance Reviews*

Date	Type of Review	Interviewer	Action Taken (if any)	Comments

Type of Review
1. Job perf. & dev.   4. Routine
2. Compensation   5. Discipline
3. Complimentary   6. Other

Promotions and Transfers*

Date of Change	Old Position and Location	New Position and Location	Employee accepted/ rejected	Position was: 1. Promotion 2. Lateral 3. Demotion	Comments

Work Schedule Changes*

Date of Change	TOTAL HOURS WORKED WEEKLY IN: (List only permanent changes in the employee's schedule) Old Schedule	New Schedule	Comments

When either full-time or part-time work is offered to an employee and it is rejected, it is very important that this be noted on the employee's application form.

Compensation Changes

This information should be properly recorded on the payroll records.

*In every case, proper records such as copies of training records, discipline-type interviews, performance reviews, promotion and transfer records, lay offs and recalls, and work schedule changes should be made a part of the employee's personnel file in addition to having the notation made on this form.

to employees—his or her credibility will rise sharply in their eyes when they know that he or she is working for their advancement.

—Posting jobs available and having a system to encourage individuals to seek higher-level jobs.

—Giving recognition to supervisors for developing and making available promotable individuals.

—Using job rotation and career clinics as a means of creating interest in other jobs and increasing talents available and as evidence of company interest in the growth of the individual.

—Designing and administering the type of human resource data system that ensures promotion of the best-qualified individuals and making certain that this is communicated to the extent that everyone knows that he or she will receive full consideration when a better job becomes available. This should also include a system of communicating with those not promoted to explain why they were passed over.

—Making certain that the system accommodates the mavericks, the highly talented, and the fast-track individuals.

THE FREEDOM TO DISCUSS MOBILITY

Although a formal system for promotions, mobility, and use of talent is necessary, the most effective method of assuring the full use of potential is the employees' relations with their supervisor and the company. They must have sufficient confidence in the supervisor, the system, and the company to discuss careers, promotions, and aspirations. In many instances, they want reassurance; they want answers; they want to know what is available and what might happen; or they just want to be able to talk about their future.

The company's most serious brain drain occurs because employees do not feel free to discuss their career interests with various levels of management. The following examples are typical of statements made to me.

"I didn't feel I could talk with my supervisor about the promotion."

"I don't think my boss would be in favor of my making the move, although it is the type of job I would really like to have."

"Please don't discuss this with my foreman; I don't think he would approve of my talking with you."

"I hope you won't discuss this with my manager, because he might hold it against me. It seems that if anyone wants a transfer or talks about a promotion, he takes it as a personal insult and says that apparently we don't like him or our job in his department."

"If I had known that I could be considered for the promotion, I wouldn't have accepted the job with the other company before coming in to resign."

"I never really understood the promotion system. It just appeared to me that most of it depended on who played up to the boss."

"It seemed that every time a better position became available someone was brought in from the outside."

The reasons employees resign and accept other jobs is that they don't have faith in the system, don't feel free to discuss the situation, or simply believe that things are not working in their favor. The company should create a climate in which every employee, regardless of level, has ready access to his supervisor and other involved management to discuss job-related concerns before dissatisfaction leads to the acceptance of another job.

PRODUCTIVE USE OF HUMAN TIME

Making maximum use of available human resources also means full utilization of time available. The following statements should provide guides for the effective use of human time.

—Ensure that employees have beneficial work to do on a continuing basis. Employees generally want to be busy all the time. Time passes faster, they feel a greater sense of contribution, and they derive more job satisfaction.

—Create the awareness that time and potential contribution are the main things the company purchases from the individual and that it is the only process through which the individual can achieve personal goals.

—Place a value on time; for the individual making $10,000, every working minute is worth approximately 17 cents.

—Communicate the uniqueness of time—that it cannot be

expanded, contracted, stored, or stopped and that the flow is never reversible. Time is highly quantifiable and is the dimension in which all change, growth, and achievement must take place.

—Analyze the availability and utilization of time in the department as carefully as the expense budget and other key influences.

—Determine the time users that are not essential; where can the amount of time used be reduced?

—Determine where better planning, organization, work flow, streamlining processes, more effective priorities, rearrangement, better scheduling, and additional training will make better use of time.

—In order to obtain better ROI from time, consider setting deadlines, alternative methods, consolidation, concentration of effort, greater delegation, elimination of details and reduction of paperwork, job discipline, managing by exception, controlling interruptions, quick feedback, time-use planners, and more realistic anticipation.

—In managing the time of others, consider improvements in training, better understanding of job methods and requirements, work planning to ensure a constant flow, availability of supervisors to solve problems and provide solutions, elimination of roadblocks and interference to productive activity, "expect and inspect," avoiding wasting time of subordinate, and planning work programs and assignments to ensure that all individuals are making a full contribution while the supervisor is away from the department.

—Identify and eliminate, or at least minimize, the effect of such time wasters as unexpected interruptions, telephone calls, meetings, reports, inadequate delegation, and the many others that usurp excessive amounts of potentially productive human time.

—Communicate that it is the company, its system, and its leadership that make available the opportunity for the full utilization of all human time purchased. Individuals are assigned to jobs, told how the job should be done, and given some indication of how much time has been allocated. Although individuals should be encouraged to suggest time-efficiency initiatives, the responsibility rests most heavily with management. Managers should set the example and provide the framework for subordinates.

BUILDING INDIVIDUAL SELF-ESTEEM

Performance and permanence often depend on job satisfaction, which in turn is significantly influenced by the self-esteem the job and the company afford the incumbent. When the job builds self-esteem in the incumbent, the individual thinks more highly of the company and is less likely to leave. Building self-esteem becomes mutually beneficial to both company and individual goals. Building self-esteem involves the following.

Treating employees as individuals and not as numbers, crowds, or classes. Calling by name, engaging in conversation, keeping promises, showing awareness of what is being done, encouraging suggestions, and demonstrating personal interest indicate the high value the company places on the individual as a human being.

Giving deserved recognition for job performance. Giving credit promptly and spontaneously, encouraging initiative and use of seldom-used talent, exercising caution in placing blame, giving appropriate recognition for effort as well as actual results, and leveling with the employee are essential ingredients of sound employee relations. I have accepted resignations from employees who gave as their main reason for leaving that they didn't feel the supervisor was leveling with them by pointing out their faults and being firm enough in bringing about their growth.

Building self-confidence. Creating confidence that the employee can succeed, taking time to listen and placing value on what the employee says, criticizing tactfully and constructively, and taking advantage of every opportunity to build self-confidence and create positive relations. At times every employee is beset with uncertainty and insecurity unless something is done to counteract this feeling.

Top performers believe in themselves, their supervisors, and the company. They arrive at this stage only if they have experienced success and believe that conditions are favorable for their continuing growth.

CREATING CONFIDENCE IN THE COMPANY

Regardless of company and supervisory effort, the employee will never know everything he or she might like to know about the things that can affect his or her job. The individual will be inclined to be distrustful about what he or she doesn't know or understand without having confidence in the good intentions and purposes of the company as it might influence him or her.

But how does a company create and maintain this type of confidence so essential to performance and retention? It consists of some major areas and many little things. For example, the individual must perceive the system as working advantageously for him, and the system must not deprive the employee of what he assumes to be achievable through the company and job. The employee should have confidence that the system is sufficiently effective to ensure his or her future security and growth opportunity and to provide for the continuity of the company. The individual has a self-interest in an efficient, growing, profitable company. The system should be seen as instrumental in providing a positive thrust toward this goal rather than as an impediment to its achievement.

MONITORING AND CONTROLLING TURNOVER

Loss of talented human resources and cost of replacement can represent a sizable expense. But it can be anticipated and controlled within acceptable limits. Turnover isn't something that happens; it is caused by internal conditions that motivate the employee to seek more attractive conditions at competitive companies.

Some turnover is healthy and desirable; it tends to decrease the cost of employee benefits and to eliminate nonproductive employees. This provides opportunity for the employment of bright, creative newcomers and opens channels for promotions. Some turnover is unavoidable for such reasons as retirement, moving out of town, health, and marriage, and some turnover becomes necessary during economic downturns or as a result of cyclical impact of product or market change.

Excessive turnover, on the other hand, can result in unacceptable replacement costs through recruitment and employment, relocation, training, and additional supervision. Too much turnover can have an adverse effect on recruiting efforts in that prospects want to know why the position is open and why the last person resigned or was discharged. Excessive turnover impacts negatively on those remaining, creating a feeling that maybe something is wrong with the company or that opportunities are better else-where. Often resignations occur in bunches, one triggering others. Turnover can place current goal achievement in jeopardy.

Although some turnover and loss of people might be acceptable and unavoidable, it is beneficial to know what loss is occurring and its effect on the company operation. The first step in managing turnover includes determining why people leave. This can be done through exit interviews, which should uncover the employee's real reasons for leaving. In many instances the official reason given the department supervisor is not the real reason for the resignation.

Questionnaires should be sent to former employees to enable them to react more objectively and honestly at a later time. In addition, a careful analysis of turnover should be made with regard to sex, age, length of service, type of job, level of position, pay grade, department, and location.

A program for reducing turnover would include corrective action, such as:

Improving screening, hiring, and job placement.

Better orientation and counseling for new employees (it is the short-term employee who is more likely to leave).

Providing more appropriate amounts and types of training and development.

Training supervisors to be better managers of people and job activities.

Improving working conditions—the physical as well as the human environment.

Ensuring that pay and benefits are competitive—conducting surveys to see that they are kept competitive.

Ensuring maximum utilization of talent and potential.

Showing greater concern for the individual.

Providing maximum involvement, interest, motivation, and satisfaction through job enrichment.

Including responsibility for turnover in every manager's position description and standard of performance.

Assigning specific overall company accountability for controlling turnover and preserving the human resource asset to a competent executive who will be judged by results.

Creating a constant awareness of the cause of and action necessary to prevent unnecessary employee turnover.

Reduced and controlled turnover can benefit efficiency, customer relations, employee relations, costs of operation, and profit. Of equal importance, it provides a deliberate program for protecting the investment already made in human resources. Once this resource is gone, so is the investment and all opportunities for future return.

The substantial investment made in acquiring the human resource asset and bringing it to acceptable productive levels merits high-priority attention to its preservation. This means a systematic management-directed program for determining what employees want from their jobs; what causes turn-ons, turn-ons-plus, turn-offs, and turnovers. Management should constantly keep in mind that employees have reasons for job dissatisfaction and resignations.

In order to ensure an ROI in human resources, programs must be designed, initiated, administered, monitored, and changed to retain the valuable human resource asset, both purchased from the outside and created through internal programs. It should be remembered that the discharge or resignation of an employee most often represents a failure and waste. The company has possibly failed in its responsibility of developing and utilizing. It might have failed to provide appropriate leadership or forms of compensation. The employee concludes that his or her career and other needs can be met better elsewhere. A discharge represents a judgment on the part of management that the individual has failed to meet the needs of the company. Separation, for whatever cause, often represents failures prior to the actual separation decision—failure on the part of the company in its initial employment, various placements, and provision of an appropriate working environment. The individual might have failed to respond satisfactorily to opportunities the company provided by giving inadequate response to training, leadership, and other requirements.

12
Effective management of human resource data

One of the most exacting tests faced by management is its ability to make proper decisions relating to its people. These decisions deal with lives and families; they border on moral implications; and many are legal in nature and could involve costly fines and public embarrassment if made improperly. In addition, most decisions involve not only immediate consequences but also long-range impact. Human decisions are precedent-setting in nature, since a decision regarding one person establishes the pattern for similar decisions. They have great economic impact on the operation and profitability of the company. Wrong versus right human decisions determine whether the enterprise achieves or misses its purpose for being in business.

Decisions regarding people cover almost the entire range of company activities. They include decisions about employment, job placement, training, promotions, transfers, pay rates, pay increases, working conditions, supervision, employee benefits, layoffs and discharges, individual qualifications, performance evaluation; and various types of personnel-related policies. People decisions are especially hazardous because of the difficulty of knowing all the influencing factors. It is relatively easy to predict the result if money is borrowed at 8 percent interest. But the greater uncertainty of consequences weighs heavily on supervisors who make decisions regarding people, especially when those decisions could result in employee dissatisfaction, resignation, or complaint to a shop steward or a government agency. They could also have a negative influence on the goals of the department and the entire company. Every human decision should, to the fullest extent possible, be mutually beneficial to both parties.

The key to making the right decisions is having the facts or data on which they are based. If facts are inaccurate, obsolete, inadequate, or distorted, they result in bad decisions. Accurate decision making depends on the opposite set of circumstances—accurate, adequate, current information. The emphasis on more effective data systems has been brought about by the increasing difficulty of including all useful information in decision making, the need for more and quicker decisions, organizational growth and changing structure, and the increasing cost of data maintenance and reporting.

It has been the necessity of finding ways to meet needs and reduce costs that has fostered the growth of electronic data systems for processing personnel information. Companies have explored and experimented with various procedures for making available the types of data needed for decision making. The systems range from simple ones to the most elaborate EDP equipment. The size or type of system is important only as it relates to system costs and its effectiveness in achieving data goals. A system should never become a goal in and of itself, but should always be viewed as a highly efficient management tool for collecting, systematizing, storing, maintaining, and retrieving information about an organization's human resources.

In order to meet the challenge of increased numbers, risks, and costs of personnel-related decisions, faster access to accurate and complete information has become essential. Organizational changes, increased technology, new trends in employee benefits and compensation, widely disbursed employee locations, legal implications, and the necessity for a more successful way to utilize an organization's human resources in a cost/effective manner have demanded new approaches to human resource data systems. But emphasis on systems should not result in its being abandoned to technicians or technical considerations. The focus must be on improved personnel administration and the benefits it can derive from using the data system. (The technical design of systems and the selection of computer-related hardware will not be covered in this chapter. Rather, the emphasis will be on the contribution of an appropriate human resource data system to solve people problems.)

SYSTEM REQUIREMENTS

Typical data systems range from records that include minimal information posted and maintained manually for a limited number of employees to the 150,000-employee system maintained at IBM headquarters as part of a dual system 360 Model 50 computer installation. This latter system maintains 108 "pieces" of human resource data on each individual in addition to about 400 data elements maintained on every individual in each divisional personnel data file.

Regardless of the size or complexity of the system, information must be accurate and creditable, kept up to date, and readily accessible to those who are authorized to use it. So that all information will have the same meaning throughout the company, it should be in uniform, standard terms. Systems for gathering and storing data should be uniform and kept as simple as possible. Overall as well as various specialized needs of departments and functional activities must be accommodated, but no more than the amount of information essential to meet company goals should be held.

The system should provide for linkage to all other systems (payroll) and departments (personnel) that must interact on a continuing basis with the data. (See Figure 11, which shows the interlinking nature of functions within the general personnel administration areas. No isolated piece of the human resource function should be planned or administered without considering its interdependent relation to various other functions.)

Over and above those requirements, the system should:

Incorporate the greatest possible efficiency and savings in the processing and use of data—and at an acceptable cost.

Make possible projections, comparisons, simulations, testing, and research regarding the various types of human resource costs and activities.

Figure 11. Interdependent nature of the human resource functions.

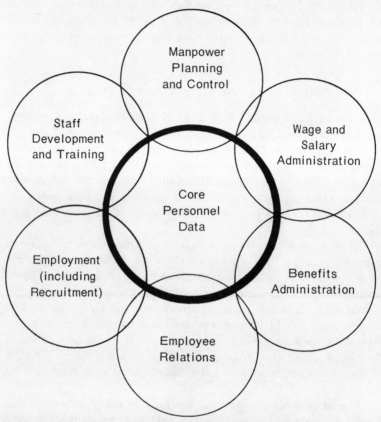

Through the courtesy of Frank F. Tetz and Towers, Perrin, Foster and Crosby, Inc., Philadelphia, Pa. Originally published by Journal of Systems Management, October, 1974.

Facilitate budgeting, planning for human resource needs, and the matching of job requirements and individual qualifications.

Have the capacity for producing various types of statements, reports, and lists required by the company and government.

Be constantly analyzed, purged, revised, and modified to meet the changing needs and goals of the enterprise.

Provide for standardized data forms, terms, storage, and usage throughout the organization.

APPLICATION AND BENEFITS OF DATA SYSTEMS

A large New England food processing company has listed the following applications for its human resource information system:

—Early identification of high-potential employees and an awareness of openings throughout the organization for these people.

—Evaluation of compensation experience for effective salary administration.

—Analysis of organizational structure and succession charting.

—Identification and evaluation of turnover.

—Analysis of recruiting approaches.

—Review and revision of benefit plans.

—Satisfaction of government reporting requirements for such agencies as the Equal Employment Opportunity Commission and the Cost-of-Living Council.

—Automatic update of other human resource-related systems, such as payroll, stock-option accounting, and profit-sharing record keeping.

The system provides management with such information as:

—Employee profiles, which display comprehensive current and historical data on employees.

—Position profiles, which provide both current and historical data on exempt positions.

—Lists of vacant authorized positions.

—Comparisons of authorized and actual manpower functions within each division.

—Displays of the corporate structure that reflect reorganization and personnel changes.[1]

An appropriately constructed and maintained human resource data system should provide these specific benefits to management:

1. Availability of substantial amounts of information about employees at a minimum cost.

2. Availability of needed information relating to compensation, location, job data, work history, performance, skills, and benefits

[1] Towers, Perrin, Foster and Crosby, Letter Number 110, October 15, 1973, Philadelphia, Pa.

from a single source and in an acceptable manner as to form, accuracy, and speed.

3. Coordination of records, reports, and various types of required information.

4. Establishment of a single source of human resource data and elimination of redundancy of collection, storage, and maintenance.

5. Availability of perpetual inventory of statistical data on human resources required for the purposes of employee selection, planning of training and development programs, expansion plan-

Figure 12. Relationship of the human resource information system to other systems.

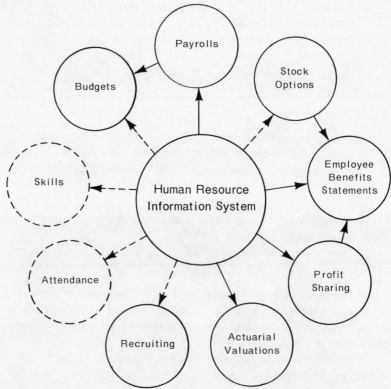

Through the courtesy of Frank F. Tetz and Towers, Perrin, Foster and Crosby, Inc. Philadelphia, Pa. Originally published by **Journal of Systems Management**, October, 1974.

ning, analysis and control of human resources, and maximum utilization of personnel competency and potential.

Figure 12 relates the core human resource data system to other systems that should be integrated into the data base. This overall emphasis should ensure that management will engage in human resource data management on a total rather than a fragmented basis.

OVERALL DATA BASE

The central core of a human resource data system is the data base. The data system, along with personal data, constitutes the factual information that serves as the basis for people decisions. Although the data base can consist of a continuously expanding list of areas, those most commonly associated with a total company data base are: [2]

Personal data.
Recruiting data.
Work experience data.
Educational data.
Compensation/work assignment data.
Evaluative/promotion data.
Length of service/layoff data.
Employee attitude/morale data.
Union membership data.
Location/contact data.
Benefit plan data.
Safety/accident data.
Data on open jobs or positions to be filled.
Characteristics of the employment environment.
Characteristics of the organization or its component parts.
Position or job history.
Labor market data.

Most companies are more successful in the construction of an adequate resource data system than they are in fully utilizing the benefits of the system after it is in operation. Expert guidance for

[2] Glenn A. Bassett and Harvard Y. Weatherbee, *Personnel Systems and Data Management*, AMACOM, 1971, p. 107.

constructing programs and for purchasing equipment are readily available. Users of the system can be instructed, but too often the system's resources and capability are neglected or misused in making crucial decisions concerning human resources. Decision makers should be reminded that ROI from the system and the large investment in human resources is dependent on the full utilization of valid information as a basis for their decisions.

TYPES OF DATA NEEDED

The Fair Labor Standards Act, along with its many amendments, and other government regulations require that certain types of data be recorded and maintained on all employees. Beyond this, various levels of management must have quick availability of pertinent information in order to make sound decisions concerning people.

Although the data might be maintained at considerable cost for the benefit of corporate goals, the individual employee also has a stake in the quick availability of accurate data concerning himself or herself and his or her relationship with the company. For example, the data system, in addition to basic types of information, should prove advantageous to the individual by having available information regarding educational background, qualifications, level of job performance, promotability, job changes and promotions, and other types of information that would help to ensure that the company has ready access to data that could enhance his or her security and career growth. If the data is properly used, the individual can be assured that the company is fully aware of his or her record and availability. Too many employees feel that the company is not aware of their qualifications and desires and that they are overlooked when promotions are made. It becomes advantageous to both company and individual ROI to have available the types of data needed to make decisions that will be most beneficial to both parties.

PERSONAL DATA BASE LIST

The following data should be included in the personal data base:

Full name.

Address, including zip code.

Date of birth.

Sex and marital status.

Social Security number.

Work location.

Salary, hours worked, and pay number.

Position title and/or code.

Date employed.

Date of last performance appraisal.

Qualifications based on education, skills, knowledge, and competency.

Names, sex, and birth dates of dependents.

Security clearance.

Physical characteristics, if pertinent.

Relocation information.

Job history with the company—promotions, transfers, training, special assignments, and special interests (possibly hobbies).

Normal retirement date.

Vested rights or benefits (increasingly important).

Salary history.

Breaks in service—for example, leaves of absence, long-term illness, military duty.

The specific types of data contained in the system should vary according to the specialized needs of the company. Certain companies and areas within the company will have needs for highly unique and specialized information. The number of data items might range from the minimum legally required to hundreds. Before data is included, it should be tested to determine whether it is legally required; whether it is needed for control purposes; whether it will aid management in its decision making, whether it will be beneficial to the individual; whether it will serve management in budgeting, forecasting, and planning; whether its benefits will justify the cost; whether it can be integrated with other data; whether it is the most efficient way to make the information available; and, most important, whether it will be used. Much of the human resource data contained in personnel files and in EDP systems is never used. The most costly and worthless data is that which is never used or is used too seldom to justify its cost.

HOW DATA WILL BE GATHERED

Where does all the data come from and how will it be brought together? A standardized procedure for bringing the data together should be designed into the initial start-up and ongoing operation of the system. Data flow is concerned initially with bringing together information needed to create the system. Once the system is operating, the concern shifts to ensuring a continuing inflow and update.

In addition to the employee himself, data is generally available from application forms, personnel and payroll records, benefits records, production and sales reports, appraisal reports, development and training reports, and unique sources as influenced by the particular individual or the special requirements of the data system.

In some instances, information is transferred directly from the source to the data system. In most instances special forms must be designed and used for the transfer of data from source to data bank. The specific type of form will be influenced by the nature of the data to be transmitted. Regardless of differences, all systems should provide for the flow of information on a "fail safe" basis. Nothing can be retrieved from the system that wasn't put in. If the promotion of Martha Smith in the accounting department was not reported, the system becomes obsolete.

Responsibility for bringing the data together and ensuring its constant flow should be assigned to specific individuals (generally the individuals responsible for operating the system). They, in turn, work back through personnel and other departments in order to get the required data.

SYSTEMATIZING DATA FOR FUTURE USE

Systematizing data begins with its end use. What will be needed and in what form? How can it best be arranged in order to have it available as needed? The storage system requirements usually determine the arrangement of reported data. The systematizing (or categories) is based on anticipation of printout demands. The arrangement of data should consider:

—Requirements of the data storage system to be used (hardware and software).

—Identification of and provision for printout of types of information needed; for example, those individuals having special qualifications continuously needed by the company (a skills inventory), normal retirement ages, and those qualified for promotion.

—Standardization of terms, codes, definitions, and data. The system should provide for the changing of all data (where necessary) into defined categories and for the editing of data received.

—The system's capacity for interfacing with all other human resource and related systems.

The question to be answered is: "What does management expect from the system?" All data should be arranged to meet this expectation. In order to do this, the data involved and the storage system must undergo a careful matchup.

STORING DATA

The storage form can vary from cards to multi-million-dollar computers. It can be manual or electronic. The sophistication and cost of the storage facility generally reflect the complexity and dynamics of the enterprise. There is obviously greater need for data utilization if the company is experiencing or anticipates growth, relocations, or other changes that will require human resource changes. Also, increased demands for reports and other types of data for compliance with government regulations increase the need for electronic storage and retrievability.

The Employee Retirement Income Security Act of 1974, which impacts on pensions, profit-sharing plans, employee insurance, and other benefits, added a new dimension to data requirements. This law requires numerous additional statistical reports: credit for breaks in service if the separated employee returns to work and continues for a certain period of time, reporting vested rights and amounts when requested by the employee, and many data-related demands that would be very difficult and expensive to meet with a purely manual system. Many consultants are now pointing out the necessity of EDP to companies with retirement plans.

The mushrooming demand for data, reports, projections, and planning information makes manual storage impractical for large companies. As stated by Carlton W. Dukes,

[the cost and type of human resource equipment will] depend primarily upon existing data processing equipment installations and expertise within a particular company. Unfortunately, few personnel departments can requisition a computer for their own purposes. In the complex, expensive world of data processing, most computer applications are devoted to financial or materials controls purposes for their economic justification. Therefore, the best approach to determining the complexity of the system to be installed is through capitalization on the existing computer installation, rather than entertaining thoughts of a new computer that is dedicated solely to personnel activities. Some equipment can be reasonably requested, especially if it is only storage capacity or a special printer or terminal device to be connected to the computer.[3]

Where computer equipment is not available in the organization, the alternatives might be to have a "stand-alone" system using minicomputers or to rent time from a computer utility that will provide not only the computer but also the terminal devices, such as video displays and printers. In addition to purely manual systems, the following computer systems are those most often used.

Punch cards, or unit-record system. This system has been in use for about 20 years and is primarily an accounting machine capable of rapidly processing many pieces of information. The system has no "memory" and fails to provide much of the capability demanded today.

Tape, or sequential-access system. This is often referred to as the second-generation computer and consists of data cards converted to magnetic tape. The system can be used for standardized sorting and printing. It is capable of providing custom reports, along with statistical calculations made possible by combining mathematical and logical operations to compare diverse values.

Disk, or direct-access system. This third-generation equipment markedly increases the amount of data that can be economically stored. It consists of magnetic tape that makes possible retrieval in any sequence rather than from beginning to end. This system also facilitates the storage, changing, and location of large numbers of data at a more reasonable cost. It operates at great speed, is capable of processing very large files, and can process several programs simultaneously.

All human resource systems of the type produced by EDP

[3] Carlton W. Dukes, *Computerized Personnel Resource Data,* AMACOM, 1971.

represent a cost that must be balanced against the benefits of alternate systems. Information systems have a continuing need for machines capable of sorting and listing, selecting and identifying, and performing statistical analyses, but second-generation computers can handle much of this. Whether to go beyond this level will probably be influenced by the equipment and expertise available in the organization, the overall demands for data, and the size of the company.

CONTINUOUSLY UPDATING THE SYSTEM

By the time a system is installed, the data is obsolete unless there is a built-in system for continuously providing for data input and update. In the typical company, changes are occurring every day. Pay increases and promotions are given. Job performance evaluations are conducted. Personal information such as address and marital status change. Employees complete training programs and periods of job orientation. Decisions made without the benefit of this current information are risky and often unjust to both the company and the individual.

Two timing systems can be used to ensure the inflow of information to the data system. The first provides for the reporting and recording of information daily as it occurs. It can be assumed that data under this system is always up to date. The second involves accumulating information and reporting it on a scheduled basis; for example, at the end of every month.

To ensure that the human resource data system will be continuously updated, management should determine, first of all, whether provisions for updating have been sufficiently built into the system and whether forms and procedures are available and are in the hands of the right people. The people responsible for reporting the information must be properly trained in recording and transmitting the data. It's also important to determine whether data is being reported accurately and according to time schedules. This can be accomplished by identifying critical results areas and checking them at regular intervals.

It cannot be assumed that information will continue to flow into the system unless there are specific provisions to make it happen. Otherwise, it will be garbled, late, or never reported. Although much of the data flows from the personnel, payroll, benefits, and training departments, significant amounts of update must come from line operating departments. These are the executives who might consider all the paperwork unnecessary. They are busy with other responsibilities. Those responsible for updating the system will need to devote special attention to ensuring the reporting of current information. If the system is permitted to become obsolete, it cannot meet the purpose for which it was designed.

PRACTICAL RETRIEVAL SYSTEM

All the effort and expense involved in the creation of a human resource data system have accomplished nothing up to this stage in its design and operation. The benefit or ROI in the system depends on the availability and use of the data. Obviously, it cannot be utilized until it is available in a usable form. This is the responsibility of the retrieval system—to make the data available quickly and in language useful to decision makers. A retrieval system must be concerned with:

Who will be authorized to have access to data. Much of the data will be highly confidential—salaries, production, sales, and future strategies.

Language or form of the retrieved data. If it comes from the system in code (numbers or symbols), it must be translated into forms usable by its ultimate client. Also, the user must follow certain rules of grammar or syntax so that the computer will understand the nature of the request.

Flexibility and selectivity of data searching. The more advanced systems enable the user to obtain only the information needed. But these systems also provide the flexibility of summary reports, multi-line listings, mailing labels, totals, cards, and detailed reports.

Manner in which the data is displayed. The retrieved information should be flagged, arranged, or otherwise highlighted in such a way that a busy executive can make maximum use of it with a minimum requirement of time.

Overall efficiency. It should operate at high speed and offer such efficiencies as the ability to produce many reports with one search and be able to select only data required to produce the report.

The retrieval system must have the capability of making available the specific types of data needed, when required, in a usable form, and at an acceptable cost. The quick availability of precise information should reduce the time and errors associated with delayed and inaccurate data. It should make possible more innovative personnel programs and plans. This will enable management to perform otherwise infeasible tasks, since complex analyses with numerous variables are available for decision making through the use of more advanced systems. And perhaps the greatest advantage and savings can be derived from the additional research, simulation, and better decision making regarding the impact of human resources on profit.

ENSURING EFFICIENT USE OF DATA

Top management should set the example by requesting and using information provided by the human resource data system. The payoff for the whole (often costly) system will be the degree to which the data is put to use for the benefit of both the enterprise and the individual. To get the most out of a system, the following points are important:

1. A searching for all needed information before decisions are made.

2. An analysis of the system's capability when a need arises for reports, research, summaries, projections, or specific information. If data is available from the system, it should be utilized before duplicating effort or seeking data from some other source.

3. A review of decisions, actions, and various activities to determine whether all available information is being fully used.

4. A requirement that requests for pay changes, promotions, and so on also incorporate all pertinent data available from the system.

5. A system of management that makes full use of all available human resource data—a factual, quantitative, objective approach to treatment of people to achieve a fair ROI from the cost of human resources.

BUILDING AND MAINTAINING A SKILLS INVENTORY

"Why didn't they consider me for the promotion? I've got better qualifications than the person they promoted." "Why do we have to go outside to fill these jobs? Don't we have people in the company who are qualified or who could be trained in a short period of time?" "I can't figure out why I never get people with the qualifications I request." "Why are we laying off people in one department and hiring new people in another department?"

These statements are fairly typical and are symptoms of inadequate or improperly utilized skills inventories. The data system should contain sufficient information to make possible a skills inventory base. Proper systematizing and keying can make this feature available when needed for discovering skills available and for matching skills with needs.

EVALUATING THE DATA SYSTEM

Even the most sophisticated electronic data system is simply a form of record keeping. It has many obvious advantages and some disadvantages over manual systems. Decisions regarding the degree of computerization and evaluation of the data system in use should include the following checkpoints.

ROI cost. Costs and benefits of a particular system should be compared with those of various other systems. Does the additional benefit justify the additional cost?

Sizing of the data system. Is it the right scale for the company and its needs? Money can be wasted if the system is too large or too complicated for the company.

Systems controls. Like any accounting or record system, there must be controls in order for the system to ensure that data-in, data-out, and data-use are controlled in accordance with guidelines established by management.

Adequate documentation. The data system should provide sufficient documentation to satisfy company and government requirements regarding employment, promotion, compensation, and various other personnel-related practices.

Systems sensitivity and flexibility. The system should provide for individually tailored reports and should be sufficiently versatile to meet the specialized needs of the company.

Updating and reliability. How often is the data in the system updated? Does the system make available both current and historical data? The system should include built-in controls and checkpoints to ensure its continuous and regular update. Consideration should be given to the rate of decay of data and purging of worthless information.

Competency of the operating staff. Is the staff professionally trained? The staff should be competent to operate the system and to make certain that data is accurate and reliable.

Security of the data. Does data security, in theory and in practice, meet the security standards set by management? Managers will not make available data that is revealed beyond the limits to which they have agreed.

Availability of professional guidance. Very few individuals concerned with supplying or using data will be experts in the operation of the system and utilization of the data. The ROI from the system and its daily usefulness might well depend on the availability of expert guidance from within the company, if available, or from an outside source, if necessary.

Interface with other systems. The data should interface smoothly and economically with other systems and with a minimum of disruption to these systems.

THE FUTURE OF HUMAN RESOURCE DATA SYSTEMS

It has been stated that information will be the number one economic resource of the future. Information processing will certainly not stand still. Research and improved techniques will make possible faster input devices, lower-cost storage, more effective retrievals, and a broader application of data. But perhaps the greatest predictable future benefit will be the interactive nature of the human resource data system with other forms of data stored and used throughout the company.

Future resource systems will provide negative reinforcement for erroneous inquiries and positive reinforcement for appropriate inquiries of the system. Key words will be in color, unique types of information will be sorted and coded, and visual profiles or graphs will be produced. Early data systems were generally just faster, more efficient methods of processing pieces of information—merely replacing manual systems with greater speed and possibly at a smaller cost. But computer manufacturers are now moving forward and discovering exciting new applications of EDP to human resources. Many companies are already using computers to print out dates of eligibility for employee benefits and automatically forwarding appropriate forms to concerned individuals, and matching employee hours with production demands. Lists of new applications are constantly emerging.

The negative or positive impact of human resource data systems, especially of the more complex computer variety, will be influenced significantly by decisions made in these major related areas:

Priorities as determined by management in the control of data.

Setting of objectives and goals relating to the data system.

Striking a balance between centralized and decentralized storage and use.

Determination of the elements that should be included in a workable system.

The extent to which the human resource data system will be integrated with other systems.

Discovery of additional uses and benefits from the system.

Success in testing, refining, improving, and economizing through use of the system.

Use of the system to engage in personnel research and meet the demands for reports from within and outside the organization.

Design and operation of a data system that provides required information at the most advantageous short- and long-range cost. The development of a plan of this type involves four steps: conceptual design, system specifications, system development, and implementation.

Simply stated, the increasing cost of human time and the crucial impact of employee relations decisions make mandatory data systems that provide management with every shred of information helpful in making decisions. Inadequate information means bad decisions. Bad decisions mean waste of human resources, dollars, and employee goodwill. Increased government regulations, demands for reports, and the necessity of anticipating future probabilities make EDP the servant that few companies can survive without. Just as the company must be efficient and competitive in its production and deliveries, so must it be competitive in designing and operating competitive human resource data systems.

13

The individual's entitlement to ROI

This is probably the most important chapter in the book. It deals with the emerging human dimension that management understands least, and it is the subject that might well determine both the continuity and future profitability of the enterprise. It is the ROI the individual employee, from lowest entry to the president, wants and feels entitled to in return for that portion of his or her life sold to the company each day.

This book has repeatedly emphasized the company's critical need for ROI in human resources. But what about the other side of the coin—what the individual wants and receives in return for his or her investment in the company? What sort of return are employees entitled to? "They're paid, aren't they?" "They're covered by employee benefits." "They've got steady jobs." "After all, they're a lot better off than many others, especially in other parts of the world. So what more do they want?"

The time has arrived when the ability of the enterprise to attract, retain and motivate people will be in direct proportion to what individuals believe they are getting in return for their contribution to the company. A job has become more than a means of earning a livelihood; it has become part of the individual's self-image and an instrument through which he or she becomes an efficient citizen. The economic climate, mores, society, inflation, individual conditioning, and educational levels have altered expectations. The trend is clear: worldwide, there is a rapidly rising psychology of expectations. Economic declines will have only a temporary influence on acceptance by the individual of lessened return. For example, in 1974 increased unemployment did not lower demands for wage increases. Employee benefits were not reduced or eliminated in order to preserve jobs. In most instances, the demands were for more pay, continuation of benefits after layoffs, and more guarantees that entitlement be fulfilled by the company. If the company failed or was unable to meet this need, individuals and groups turned for help to various levels of government.

It is not the purpose of this chapter to moralize regarding rightness or wrongness of expectations, on either the part of the company or the individual; the purpose is to advise management to accept the fact that individual ROI is very much alive and growing. Success in enabling individuals to experience acceptable ROI is the number one challenge confronting management. Individuals will have the education, the intelligence, and the ability to make the company successful, but whether this potential is applied for the maximum benefit of the company will depend on individual ROI.

INCREASING AWARENESS OF INDIVIDUAL RIGHTS

Many factors have brought the rights of the individual and the impact of these rights into the boardrooms and leadership training programs of every major corporation. Explanations for this phenomenon would certainly include:

1. Unions and their representation for the rights of the individual.

2. Government regulations with their many tentacles of influence: entitlement of minimum wages, overtime, workman's compensation, safety, equal pay and promotional opportunities, rights for minorities and protected age groups, Social Security, unemployment compensation, and many more.

3. Requirements that individuals be informed of their rights regarding government requirements, rights to organize, rights to lodge complaints, where and how to complain, and protection from job loss if complaints are made.

4. A liberated society that approves of pressure and special-

interest groups—where company loyalty and attachment are less decisive than the force of individual entitlement.

5. Individuals who are willing to confront management regarding rights, expectations, and conditions.

6. Lessened fear of job loss and the consequences of unemployment because of the availability of other jobs and benefits for those unemployed.

7. Perhaps, most importantly, the influence of all these factors in changing the lifestyle and total expectations of individuals in return for their services.

Many of these influences elevate the dignity of the individual, creating a sense of equality and wholeness; many are the application of good personnel practices and management; and many result in long-range benefit to the company. It is unfortunate that, in some instances, corporate leadership fails to demonstrate the initiative in providing for these individual benefits and waits, instead, for legal coercion.

The financial and organizational consequences of these individual rights can prove highly significant. Often, whole compensation and employee benefits plans must be changed. Employment and promotional procedures must be restructured. Physical changes in the work environment have to be made. Job performance evaluations, promotional procedures, corrective interviews, and justification for discharge must be restructured. Leadership must be retrained to be more humanistic, and yet candid at the same time. Supervisors must be made aware of individual rights, whether legal or the result of changing expectations. Supervisors must be trained to cope with the new demands brought about by individual ROI expectations.

CHANGING CONCEPTS ABOUT WORK

It is of critical importance that management become aware of society's and the individual's changing concept about work. Something vital to the company is happening; either management will become aware and respond in an acceptable manner, or it will continue to ignore these dynamic forces, at its own peril.

Employees have been told that they are important. Their jobs and what they do at work are of critical importance to the company. They have been led to believe that the traditional work ethic is in effect—that hard work and increased contribution will result in more pay and enhanced growth opportunity. But unfortunately, in the minds of many employees, and too often in actual company practices (or malpractices), it just doesn't work out that way.

Consider the following emerging attitudes toward work and companies:

The blue-collar worker . . . is not a hard hat or an Archie Bunker, but a hard worker who is underpaid, undervalued, unhappy.[1]

While negotiations over wages and fringe benefits seem to have received the lion's share of attention in the past few decades, considerable interest has been displayed over the past year in our magazines, newspapers, and other media in the quality of working life.[2]

Our nation is being challenged by a set of new issues having to do, in one way or another, with the quality of life. This theme emerges from the alienation and disenchantment of blue-collar workers; from the demands of minorities for equitable participation in "the system"; from the search by women for a new identity and by the quest of the aged for a respected and useful social role; from youth who seek a voice in their society; and from almost everyone who suffers from the frustrations of life in a mass society.[3]

Work offers economic self-sufficiency, status, family stability, and an opportunity to interact with others in one of the most basic activities of society. Consequently, if the opportunity to work is absent, or if the nature of work is dissatisfying (or worse), severe repercussions are likely to be experienced in other parts of the social system.[4]

Many workers at all occupational levels feel locked in, their mobility blocked, the opportunity to grow lacking in their jobs, challenge missing from their tasks. Young workers appear to be committed to the institution of work as their elders have been, but many are rebelling against the anachronistic authoritarianism of the workplace. Minority workers similarly see authoritarian work settings as evidence that society is falling short of its democratic ideals. Women, who are looking to work as an additional source of identity, are being frustrated by an opportunity structure that confines them to jobs damaging to their self-esteem.[5]

[1] Andrew Levison, *The Working Class Majority* (New York: Coward, McCann, and Geoghegan, 1975).

[2] Report of a Special Task Force to the Secretary of Health, Education, and Welfare, "Work in America" (Cambridge, Mass., and London, England: The MIT Press, 1973).

[3] Ibid.   [4] Ibid.   [5] Ibid.

The economic and societal importance of work has dominated thought about its meaning, and justifiably so: a function of work for any society is to produce and distribute goods and services, to transform "raw nature" into that which serves our personal needs and desires. Far less attention has been paid to the personal meaning of work, yet it is clear from recent research that work plays a crucial and perhaps unparalleled psychological role in the formation of self-esteem, identity, and a sense of order.[6]

Working is, "A search, too, for daily meaning as well as daily bread, for recognition as well as cash, for astonishment rather than torpor; in short, for a sort of life rather than a Monday through Friday sort of dying." [7]

Work, for the modern employee, must be more than the price of economic survival. It must take him or her beyond entrapment in a dull, noisy, dirty, unchallenging work prison. A human being wants psychic as well as economic compensation. Work becomes a source of either human gratification or deprivation. The employee has visions and expectations of what the physical and human work environment could be.

Visionary? Hardly! This is what employee satisfaction and motivation are all about. Perhaps the job and the company will never become the perfect Camelot for either executive or worker, but there are ample practical opportunities to move toward the ideal. When the company makes these opportunities available to the individual, he or she is remotivated to make a greater contribution to the goals of the company.

RECONCILING COMPANY AND INDIVIDUAL NEEDS

Rather than conflicting, company and individual needs should be mutually reinforcing. The company cannot achieve its goals without capable people and their contribution. Individual employees cannot fill their needs for jobs, pay, promotions, security, job growth, and job satisfaction without jobs. When there is a conflict between individual needs and those of the company, usually the reason is inadequate understanding or unreasonable expectations from either party. It is possible that the company expects

[6] Ibid.
[7] Studs Terkel, *Working* (New York: Pantheon Books, a Division of Random House, 1974).

too much and compensates too little; it is conceivable that the individual makes unreasonable demands as payment for time on the job as compared with actual contribution.

When either company or individual makes unacceptable demands, or either fails to understand the other's position, inevitable conflict and negative consequences occur. This vitally affects the achievement ability of the company and deserves far more attention than it receives in most organizations. Inadequate effort is devoted to identifying what individuals expect from their jobs. Almost no effort is given to determining what a reasonable profit is in relation to providing for the expectations of employees. Also, very little time or attention is given to explaining the company's financial position, its heavy tax burden, and its need for retained profits to provide for future growth and enlarged opportunity for the individual.

Management is well advised to devote far more attention to determining employee expectations; in establishing reasonable compensation systems (pay, benefits, and psychic satisfaction); in enabling individuals to achieve their ROI; and in ensuring that these are adequately communicated. It has been my experience that most individual employees, regardless of level, are reasonable regarding expectations, if they believe that the company can be trusted and is leveling with them. It is certain that "canned" communications or bulletin board notices won't accomplish this goal. Rather, it is dependent on one-to-one personal relationships— supervisor talking directly with the supervised.

PURSUING MUTUAL GOALS

Reconciling possible conflict of interest can be achieved by:

—The company's awareness of and response to employee expectations. Those that cannot be met should be carefully explained.

—Recognition on the part of the individual that his or her self-interest is tied to the success of the company, that its success depends on his or her contribution.

—The creation and maintenance of mutual trust, based on awareness of mutual interests and the contribution each must make to the success of the other.

—Acceptance by the company of its responsibility for clarifying and communicating company activities in an honest and open manner so that the employee will be willing to accept what is being transmitted. (This position assumes that the company has its financial house in order, that the company is being prudently managed, and that it has nothing to hide.) This explanation should, if appropriate, clarify the cyclical nature of profits and emphasize that retention of some financial reserves can ease an economic downturn for the employee as well as the company.

ROOTS OF EMPLOYEE DISCONTENT

Why do employees feel deprived when they are working in a modern healthy physical environment and receiving the best compensation and treatment in history? Why do they feel that their ROI is inadequate and disappointing? Why is the greatest discontent in the non-monetary areas of job satisfaction and psychic income? Why has job alienation led to contempt for the "hand that feeds"?

Robert Berghash, president of Shield Manufacturing, Inc., stated:

Many work situations offer little or no feeling of personal fulfill-ment, and people are restless and dissatisfied with their positions—they have not advanced properly, they are not paid fairly, they are not treated well, there is no meaningful challenge—all adding up to a general feeling of being cogs in a wheel. They feel trapped and frus-trated in their work situation and see no other place to go. They need the pay to survive, or at least in order to keep going. They are often angry because they are not receiving some magic ingredient from their work situation. Each day they leave with an empty feeling that they have been cheated out of something.[8]

When this occurs, the result is shoddy output, high absenteeism, and high turnover. Studs Terkel, in his introduction to *Working*, states:

For the many, there is hardly concealed discontent. The blue-collar blues is no more bitterly sung than the white-collar moan. "I'm a machine," says the spot-welder. "I'm caged," says the bank teller, and

---

[8] Robert Berghash, *Investment in People, A Small Business Perspective*, AMACOM, N.Y., 1974, p. 5.

echoes the hotel clerk. "I'm a mule," says the steelworker. "A monkey can do what I do," says the receptionist. "I'm less than a farm imple-ment," says the migrant worker. "I'm an object," says the high-fashion model. Blue collar and white call upon the identical phrase: "I'm a robot." . . . The drones are no longer invisible or mute. Nor are they exclusively of one class. Markham's Man with the Hoe may be Ma Bell's girl with the headset.[9]

Social scientists emphasize that jobs have been made too routine and have been oversimplified and denuded and allowed to decay. Is everybody unhappy? Are they whimpering, spoiled children who ought to appreciate what they've got and stop com-plaining? What is the permeating source of the discontent that is for real and has such vital impact on individual companies, society in general, and the whole economic system?

Various authorities have described discontent as existing when individuals feel they are unable to control their immediate work processes. They fail to develop a sense of purpose and function that connects their activity to the overall purpose of the company. They fail to see how their effort makes life better for society, and they fail to derive from their work activity a mode of personal self-expression. The work structure denies them the humanness experienced by the entrepreneur, the hobbyist, the painter, and the teacher. They want more from life (work being a major part of it) than they are presently experiencing. They are fearful and anxious that they are missing something vital that can never be recovered. Maybe it's not out there in the business and industrial work, but then it might be.

Roots of discontent and disappointment stem from the follow-ing factors.

Increased educational levels. Increased education means better informed and more intelligent employees who have elevated their expectation sights.

Affluence and lifestyles. The American way of life—the good life, as depicted by magazines and TV—means cars, homes in suburbia, leisure, travel, boating, camps and education for children, and bodily comforts.

Desire to control one's own destiny. Slavery is supposed to be ancient history. The next generation does not have to be trapped

[9] Studs Terkel, op. cit.

in the work drudgery of their parents. They have been led by society to believe that each individual has the right to control his or her destiny and to take from life (including job) what is needed to provide the type of existence the individual wants.

Environmental influences. Educational and religious institutions have promoted the dignity of the individual. Government has passed laws and created agencies to guarantee individual entitlement. Public media has condemned injustice and highlighted "rights," whether on the job or in the consumer marketplace.

Our society, our government, and our lifestyles have pictured what the good life can be like, both on and off the job. Individuals have been led to believe that they are entitled to this type of life for themselves and their families. If it is not realized, it must be someone's fault—there has to be a scapegoat. This might become the politician or the government; but too often it becomes the job and the company, which are more visible and closer at hand.

In coping with employee expectations, companies should recognize the potential of their very positive benefit. It is the need to achieve expectations that causes individuals to want jobs, to want more money, and to respond to conditions that make them available. It is employee demands for cars, homes, travel, leisure, and comforts that have created vast new markets. Prudent management will recognize that rapidly rising employee expectations make available the opportunity they must have to attract and motivate employees and to find markets for increasing quantities of goods and services. Henry Ford recognized that cars couldn't be sold until employees made enough money to buy them.

UNDERSTANDING INDIVIDUAL EXPECTATIONS

What do employees really expect? Attitudes toward work and employee expectations have changed so radically that there is a serious and dangerous gap between management and employee thinking. This shifting work lifestyle applies to all ages, races, and sexes. Certain groups have felt more historically deprived and have been more aggressive and visible with their demands, but they represent a consensus of what most individuals want. Current and future employees, regardless of age or level in the company, will regulate their contribution in accordance with the company's success in meeting their needs in these areas:

1. Fair pay and reasonable employee benefits.
2. A job that is interesting, challenging, and stimulating.
3. A job that makes full use of the intelligence, skill, and ability of the individual.
4. Leadership that is reasonably flexible and understanding.
5. A job that awards pay and promotions on merit and not personal bias.
6. A work environment that is safe and defined, but one that still permits some innovation and individual creativity in how results will be achieved.
7. Recognition by supervisors and management when a job has been well done.
8. At least a measure of self-determination and control over one's own work activity.
9. Evidence of progress: delegation of additional responsibility, more pay, promotion, and so forth.
10. An experience of human affirmation as expressed through job satisfaction based on personal achievement.
11. A social environment on the job that is pleasing and stimulating and meets the need to belong.
12. Evidence that personal time, talent, and life are not being wasted.

In short, the employee expects to be treated as an important human being. He or she expects to make full use of his potential for his own ROI, as well as for that of the company. If the individual does not receive expectations to an acceptable degree, it will be reflected in lessened effort and other symptoms of general job disenchantment.

THE COMPANY'S RESPONSIBILITY
FOR PSYCHIC INCOME

Is the employee at fault for his or her surly attitude and poor production, or is the company at fault for failing to provide a positive climate? It should be recognized that the employee believes that it is within the power of the company to provide what he or she wants from the job—that the company can really meet employees' needs if it chooses to do so.

Significant steps that management needs to take in order to provide psychic income include the following.

1. Redesign of jobs to make them more meaningful. Every effort should be made to enrich the work experience by providing maximum variety, completion of a total task, delegation of responsibility, and a feeling that the individual can have some impact on the work activity.

2. Analysis and restructuring of most management and supervisory training programs. Dr. Robert Pearse found that only 42 percent of top management and 46 percent of middle management considered the training they had received through in-house or out-of-house programs to be useful in carrying out their daily leadership responsibilities. Both top and middle management wanted improved training in communication, conflict management, handling problem employees, improving individuals and work groups, time management, and effective decision making.[10] Many of these newer, specialized needs are not included in traditional supervisory skills-building courses. Yet, increasingly, leaders want exposure to motivational and behavioral science theories that can be applied on the job. They work with employees daily and are aware of the gap in providing for changing expectations. They recognize their own inadequacies in paying the psychic income needed.

3. Analysis of the impact of company traditions, policies, and communications. How out of date are many of these, as compared with current expectations and thinking? Obsolete frameworks often exist because the president remembers only what was important when he or she was young and just starting out in the company.

4. Research of what is happening in the company as it might relate to employee expectations: turnover rate, absenteeism, grievances, unmet goals, vacant higher positions without internal candidates to fill them, and sub-par job performance ratings.

5. Surveys to determine what employees want in relation to what they feel they are not getting. Decisions must then be made to determine what response can and should be made.

[10] Robert F. Pearse, *Manager to Manager: What Managers Think of Management Development,* AMACOM, 1974, p. 28.

It is management's awareness and initiative that prove decisive in meeting employee expectations. Total blame for employee shortcomings seldom belongs entirely on the employee's shoulders. If management fails to recognize and respond to this reality, ROI in human resources will not be realized.

THE INDIVIDUAL'S CONTRIBUTION TO ROI

I do not mean to imply that the company is totally responsible for the individual's ROI and that the individual has no involvement in the matter. The company can provide an ideal work environment, and still some individuals will fail to achieve job satisfaction. The company can make available identical physical and human conditions to all employees, but fulfillment will vary greatly with individuals. The individual who sits back and waits to be spoon-fed from the company's bottomless bounty will experience disenchantment with results and end up blaming the company.

The individual must provide some vital ingredients to the equation:

1. His presence on the job on a regular and dependable basis.

2. Willingness to participate in company training and development programs.

3. A cooperative responsive attitude toward the company and supervisors. The employee doesn't have to agree with everything that is being done, but disagreement that jeopardizes his or her performance and relations on the job will diminish his or her ROI.

4. Willingness to work within the company work-activity framework with no more variance than management will accept. To go beyond this point interferes with job security and ability to do the job.

5. Response to the career opportunities made available by the company, as represented by merit pay increases and promotions, by engaging in the type of job performance and achieving results that deserve management recognition and approval.

6. Willingness to make maximum use of time, talents, and potential for job contribution.

Too few employees believe that their self-conceived deprivation might be the result of their own shortcomings. There is no contention that an enterprise is a totally objective institution, that it ever will be, or that it is possible to reward employees on a precisely mathematical basis. But the company generally attempts to reward according to merit, and the employee must recognize that the ROI he or she expects for his or her time on the job will be significantly influenced by his or her own input.

A MODEL FOR MUTUAL ROI

High ROI expectation on the part of the employee is the best thing that can happen to the company. Desire for a larger amount of return by the employee is the root of ambition. Unambitious, unresponsive employees make little contribution to company goals. On the average, their expectations are lower. But the fast-track individual, who has high expectations, is the source of contribution vitally needed for company success.

John W. Gardner believes that the pursuit of highest obtainable goals is a basic right of the human spirit and a fundamental part of the American system. He states:

The release of human potential, the enhancement of individual dignity, the liberation of the human spirit—those are the deepest and truest goals to be conceived by the hearts and minds of the American people. And those are ideas that sustain and strengthen a great civilization—if we believe in them, if we are honest about them, if we have the courage and the stamina to live for them.[11]

In pursuing these goals, he feels that the free enterprise system and individual companies will be serving one of the highest needs of man and society. He added:

Of all the ways in which society serves the individual, few are more meaningful than to provide him with a decent job. . . . It isn't going to be a decent society for any of us until it is for all of us. If our sense of responsibility fails us, our sheer self-interest should come to the rescue.[12]

Individual ROI entitlement, completely apart from union, government or group representation, heralds a new era in the history of work. It signals the arrival of individual rights, because it is

[11] John W. Gardner, *No Easy Victories* (New York: Harper and Row, 1968), p. 16.
[12] Ibid.

both just and right. It means the late, but final, arrival of Adam Smith's notion in 1776 that management will treat employees well, because to do so will result in better work. The futurists are seeing a movement from today's professional, electronic era to one of human concern.

The future humanistic era might be characterized by placing all employees (blue collar as well as executive) on regular salary. Time clocks may be eliminated and replaced by "flexitime" (requiring employees to work a prescribed number of hours per day, but allowing them flexibility to choose their hours of work). The emphasis will be on pay for quantity and quality of tasks rather than quantity of time.

A model for mutual ROI should include:

—Recognition by company and employee of the individual's reserve capability for making a greater contribution.

—Creating opportunities for increasing mutual ROI, based on understanding, cooperation, and contribution of appropriate input by both company and employee.

—Acceptance by company management and individual supervisor that there is a moral obligation to bring about the success of people and to enable them to experience a sense of maximum ROI in return for that portion of their lives (time) that the company purchases. No corporation should ever take this responsibility lightly. Neither society nor employee will tolerate disregard for human dignity, status, fair treatment, and opportunity for job satisfaction.

—Recognition that individuals will provide the creative and innovative margin for company superiority only when it is sought, encouraged, and rewarded.

The concept of individual ROI entitlement versus company concern for ROI will shape company policies and leadership success for the foreseeable future. It is the valid presence of the humanistic age. It applies equally to all levels of personnel. The highly educated executive might have greater ROI expectations than the blue-collar employee, but each is concerned about his or her own reward concept. This concept enables the achievement of human dignity. Self-fulfillment has become a predominant motivational force and therefore deserves greatly increased management attention. Personal affirmation through work will become a goal placed in the corporate plan, along with financial goals. Obsolescent versus futuristic management will depend largely on success in providing for individual ROI. The continuity and future profitability of the enterprise will hinge largely on the success of this achievement.

14

Strategy for implementing and administering the human resource plan

Up to this point we have dealt primarily with human resource planning—theory, organizing, putting it down on paper, and constructing a program for ROI in human resources. But will it fly? Hundreds of millions of dollars were spent in developing and building a supersonic transport plane, but the project was abandoned before the plane flew or could be used to carry passengers. A major retail store spent more than $100,000 and countless hours of management time in working with consultants and educators on a two-year employee morale survey. The project failed to achieve its goal and became so cumbersome that it was terminated.

A primary responsibility of management is to judge and determine what is important to the success of the enterprise and what isn't; to determine what will work and what won't; to determine what is practical and economical in relation to cost and what isn't; to evaluate ROI in plants, equipment, and in human resources; and to find better, more effective ways for ensuring a prudent ROI in all areas of company involvement.

Management accountability becomes especially critical in coping with the problems, the costs, and the wide-ranging impact of human resources. Neither the cost nor the consequences can be ignored—to do so jeopardizes the continued existence of the enterprise. But finding right solutions is especially complicated and deceptive. The decision to build a new plant can involve a clear-cut type of logic and determination. An architect and builder can be employed, costs can be accurately computed, and results can be predicted. Solutions to people problems are more complex, answers less clear, and the effect more difficult to predict. The search for better, more predictable answers in the human resource arena is the whole purpose of ROI human resource planning. But before it will aid in making a profit and a human relations contribution, it must be implemented correctly. Then, in order to continue its effectiveness, human resource planning must be administered on an organized, flexible basis. It must have sufficient structure to ensure its understanding and success and at the same time it must be flexible enough to meet specialized needs as they arise.

APPLYING PROFESSIONAL EXPERTISE
TO PLANNING AND IMPLEMENTATION

No one ever said that planning and working with people is easy. There has been no claim that effective human resource planning can be done without the application of the highest degree of professional management expertise. In fact, there are fewer real experts (maybe there are none) available for truly professional human resource planning than there are in most other disciplines. Companies generally achieve the results they deserve—that is, what they are willing to pay for in resources and effort. Both top management and staff should fully recognize that effective human resource planning is one of the most complex and demanding activities in which the company can engage. It involves incorporating intangibles and variables into a formal program that seeks to provide well-defined guidelines for action. It seeks to ensure mutual ROI benefits to both company and individual. It must comply with government regulations, profit objectives, and employee relations requirements. Its purpose is to move from what has too often been a chaotic waste of both company and individual potential to a programmed system for forecasting probabilities and ensuring achievement of all goals related to the human resources of the enterprise.

Professionalism in human resource planning and operation should include:

Expertise in the planning process. Professional direction should be available within the company or from outside sources to ensure that all pertinent aspects of short- and long-range planning have been utilized.

Knowledgeable input and direction of the organizing process. Critical decisions are involved in the following areas:

The number of layers of management needed.

Reporting relationships as indicated by organizational charts.

Span of authority—number of positions and functions, and which ones will report to each executive.

Allocation of duties, responsibilities, and authority as specified by the position description.

Clarification of functions and responsibilities of staffs, committees, and other involved groups.

Allocation of financial resources, budgets, and facilities to various functional units.

Agreement on production, sales, and other operating results for each unit.

Professional administration and operation. How skilled will the builders of the program be? Will training and individual guidance be provided where needed? Those who administer the plan on a daily basis need expertise in the various administrative responsibilities involved.

The construction and use of effective controls and standards. I have instructed hundreds of high-level executives in the writing and use of controls and standards. These groups have included company presidents and executives of all levels with long histories of varied experience. Yet in no instance have I found anyone knowledgeable or skilled in preparing performance standards who had not been through the experience before. This has proved to me that if managers are expected to write effective controls and standards in connection with human resource planning, they must be appropriately trained.

Strategy for ensuring the success of human resource planning must certainly make provision for the input of highly skilled professional managers. Training and skills development should be available for those who need it. The American Management Associations is perhaps the most widely recognized organization devoted almost exclusively to the development of professional management. Publications, guides, and specific types of literature are available for purchase or from local libraries. Many professional associations, universities, and other resources are available to offer assistance. Also, numerous management consultants provide the guidance and training required for the implementation of professional management throughout the enterprise.

ENSURING MANAGEMENT INVOLVEMENT AND SUPPORT

A prerequisite for human resource planning, and especially its implementation and administration, must be the involvement and support of top management. Implementation probably means doing some things differently—making responsibility for human costs part of every supervisor's job, scheduling work according to ROI need, and providing for the retention of employees and for the maximum use of time available. Administration might mean new types of criteria for promotions and transfers, job performance evaluations, and more accurate accountability for human time purchased. Change often encounters resistance. It raises the question of whether the change is just another gimmick of a staff specialist or whether it has the full involvement, support, and backing of top management. You will win the support of top management in the following manner:

1. Identifying precisely the major cost and far-reaching influence of human resources and involving top management in this determination.

2. Providing guidance and leadership in developing the human resource plan.

3. Make certain that top management understands the plan, believes in it, and is willing to make use of the plan in its own area. This sets the pattern for all other executives. It is difficult for a lower-level executive to refuse participation and support if the top executive is already engaged in the activity being considered.

4. Obtaining a commitment from top management to embrace the plan as its own, not that of a planning specialist, and to communicate it to everyone on that basis.

5. Interact with management to obtain its continuing commitment and support in the day-to-day operation of the plan; without this support the plan will fail.

6. Be willing to alter the plans as requested by top management. It should be obvious that this will be done, but creators of plans become so enamored of their own creations that they foot-drag when it comes to making requested changes.

It can be assumed that management will be in favor of the plan if it has been convinced that the plan will result in a more efficient and profitable operation. Convincing management becomes a test of the skills of those who designed and are administering the plan.

MAKING THE PLAN WORK

Strategy is required both in deciding how to best achieve the human resource planning goals and in making the plan work. Those responsible for human resource planning should carefully map tactics for making the plan work successfully. Letting things happen will only assure failure. The plan, no matter how perfect, will not accomplish the intended purpose unless it is carried through to completion.

Strategy planning should not be a one-time consideration. Often, careful strategy is devised for selling and implementing a human resource plan but then it is forgotten. Months later disillusionment sets in and everyone wants to know what happened to the plan. Was the plan no good to begin with? What went wrong? Effective planning requires built-in, continuous strategy in relation to opportunity and changes in the internal and external environment. Strategy should involve decentralization and delegation to the most appropriate extent. The human resource plan should meet certain basic needs on a continuing basis, and strategy should cause this to take place. See that it is internally consistent and that it makes proper use of all available human resources. It should also have an appropriate time horizon.

Strategy involves a willingness to do complete staff work so that the plan is logical, supported by adequate factual data, and includes all necessary tools. You must be willing to schedule meetings with key executives to explain the program and obtain their support for it, and to train, instruct, coach, and otherwise work with implementing supervisors to make it as easy as possible for them to initiate and continue the plan. Finally, you must provide leadership for evaluating results, suggesting alterations, and encouraging executives to experience a sense of achievement in making the plan work.

SEEKING AND IMPLEMENTING BEST SOLUTIONS

Managers should *want* to find the best human solutions, although this is not always true. Too often, if that solution involves change or requires a different job activity, resistance is encountered. The whole purpose of research and development, industrial engineering, and work efficiency studies is to find better answers. This should be equally true in the search for better answers in the people end of the business.

There should be an awareness that a better solution is needed, that there is excessive human resource waste when employee turnover exceeds x percent. Performance goals are not being met when positions are vacant too long and when training fails to produce productive workers. Once there is conviction that better answers are needed, there should be a willingness to seek the best solutions.

The ROI human resource plan should make available to line managers the best solutions to their people problems and opportunities. Various alternatives should be examined, tested, and considered. If the advocated human resource program does not provide the best solution, then it is wrong and should be changed. But before a human resource plan can be implemented and operated successfully, there should be a genuine awareness on the part of operating managers that there is a need for better answers and that the human resource plan has the most reasonable potential for providing them.

A TOTAL HUMAN RESOURCE PLAN "BY DESIGN"

If the plan is to be total, it must encompass all pertinent human resource activities and concerns. My decision to write a book entitled *Managing by Design—for Maximum Executive Effectiveness* stemmed from a firm conviction, based on experience, that management will be no better than the design created for its operation.[1] Small businesses may operate without formal structure, and it is true that some businesses of all sizes are overformalized. But the quality of the blueprint becomes decisive in determining what the house will be like. The blueprint and understanding of both the total management structure and its various parts will have a great impact on what management does and accomplishes. This is especially true regarding human resources. The concept of total human resource planning and ROI is newer and less familiar than construction, production, and sales planning. However, the need for a total plan is just as vital to success in the human resource part of the business.

Too often a plan, especially a human resource plan, neglects vital influences. For this reason, the plan should be formalized in writing and tested, and strategy should be included for its implementation and administration. A plan of this type will be more acceptable to line managers and employees. If it is visible and if it can demonstrate mutual benefit, it has a much better chance for support and successful operation.

A SYSTEMATIC, LOGICAL, DETAILED PLAN

The plan must be really workable. Is it too theoretical, or does it deal with the real world in which employees, supervisors, and managers live? Managers are paid to produce results. They must be practical; they want tools that are readily usable and that will produce benefits right now. If the plan is to receive enthusiastic cooperation and support during implementation, it must:

1. Provide logical, acceptable solutions to the overall human resource problems and to the daily needs of managers.

[1] Ray A. Killian, *Managing by Design—for Maximum Executive Effectiveness,* AMACOM, 1968.

2. Encompass a system that is systematic, perpetuating, and reasonably simple to administer.
3. Provide sufficient how-to details and guides to ensure its understanding and ease of implementation.
4. Include forms, worksheets, examples, and other tools necessary to make it work.
5. Require a reasonable cost of time, attention, and money to operate. The cost added (or offset from other sources) should be justifiable by increased production, efficiency, or long-range benefit.
6. Be comprehensive enough to include all appropriate human resource considerations.

If the manager is expected to support the plan, he or she must be sufficiently informed about all its aspects to be convinced that it will work. The manager should have, or develop, the leadership skills demanded by the plan in order to put it into action. But the plan itself must be a reasonable instrument and roadmap for arriving at human resource solutions.

MONITORING AND CONTROLLING THE PLAN

How will you know whether the plan is working, taking root, growing? Is progress toward goals on schedule? Progress can be determined by monitoring and controlling the plan. Ideally, the plan should have a built-in system of continuous controls that ensure conformity throughout the period of time involved. Establishing control involves decisions regarding:

What to control—what to measure. What is considered critical, or what indicates unacceptable deviations from progress? For example: production results, employee turnover, staffing success, and payroll cost are typical yardsticks.

How to measure progress. What measuring instruments, numbers, criteria will be used to measure progress and deviation from expectation? For example: appropriate reports and computer print-outs will provide evidence of achievement in relation to expectation.

When will progress be measured? Typically, this might be at the end of every month, at the end of every quarter, or annually. In critical situations, it might be as frequent as daily or hourly.

Truly effective monitoring and controls must make provisions for:

—Monitoring and reporting of progress and results at strategic points.

—Controlling through the use of standards and exceptions. The use of performance standards can be the most effective technique for ensuring expected results. Written performance standards for all positions concerned with the implementation of the human resource plan should contain specific result expectations. Monitoring and feedback should reveal whether these standards are being achieved. If performance standards are properly written, and if they are being achieved, it should be safe to conclude that the plan is on track.

—"A stitch in time" preventive monitoring and controls designed to keep things on the track. It is much easier, less disruptive, and less expensive to follow this reasoning than to have to forcefully put things back on track.

—Exception reporting. Often it is not the things that are going according to plan that need management attention but rather the exceptions, or those activities and results that deviate from the plan.

—Interpretation of what deviation from plan means. How serious is it? What corrective action is called for?

—The type of motivation and reinforcement that promotes progress and cooperation with the plan.

—Taking the corrective actions that the standards, monitoring, feedback, and controls indicate should be taken.

Controls should be designed to direct the delegation and application of all human resources of the organization in a manner that will maximize the probability of achieving their predetermined objectives, as indicated by the plan. Properly implemented standards and controls should ensure this result.

MEASURING RESULTS

Proof of the value of the human resource concept and planning will be the results produced. What results did the plan promise to produce? Are they being achieved? A checklist for measuring results should include:

1. A comparative analysis of the total cost of human time. What impact has human resource planning had on cost?

2. An analysis of human resource supply and demand. Are needs anticipated far enough in advance? Are the right people being employed and promoted, on the basis of the number of successes versus failures following job placement? Is the lack of qualified employees interfering with result achievement?

3. The extent to which people are being improved through training and development. What percentage of employees was engaged in some meaningful improvement program last year? To what extent did skills-building programs increase performance and results? How many became qualified for promotions as the result of company development programs?

4. The motivational response of all employees, top to bottom, as indicated by performance ratings and performance results.

5. The extent to which all skills and potential possessed by employees are being fully utilized for the benefit of both the company and the individual.

6. The quality of leadership and supervision as indicated by turnover, productivity, morale, absenteeism, and cooperative climate.

Results should be critically tested. The company and the individual are engaged in an activity that is supposed to produce mutual benefit. The expectations as represented by numbers, percentages, dollars, changes, and trends should be analyzed. If the human resource plan is not achieving its goal, then changes should be made.

RESEARCH AND COMPARISON

Base strategy on factual knowledge—on results and not on rumors or assumptions. What is happening regarding the plan? What is the plan causing to be done in a better way? What is the plan really accomplishing? Answers to these questions are available only through research and comparison. The whole plan and its identifiable parts should be subjected to intensive research designed to test effectiveness.

Research findings and operating results should be compared with those in other companies. Are programs in other companies achieving better results? Does comparison show that certain phases of the manpower planning process are more effective in other companies? How does the rate of employee turnover compare? What about the number of units produced or sold per hour? What is the gross profit margin on units sold?

These are the types of "bottom line" answers that management is entitled to if human resource planning is to have its support. Those concerned with human resource planning (probably everyone in the company) must have faith in its purpose, its benefit, its progress, and its ultimate result. Strategy for eliciting and retaining every employee's vital support must be based on hard facts—quantitative results that can be proved. This is the only type of strategy that has any reasonable expectation of success.

CONTINUOUS REFINEMENT AND IMPROVEMENT

Every corporate activity should be in a constant process of improvement. This is especially true regarding the rapidly changing and vitally impacting world of human resources. Obsolescence occurs as rapidly as change unless adjustments are made. Many internal and external forces are at work, making changes in the plan necessary. These forces might include levels of employment, government regulations and court decisions, advanced training and development, significant changes in company planning, and inflation.

ACCOUNTABILITY FOR HUMAN
RESOURCE PLANNING

A competent executive should be assigned the specific responsibility of making certain that the whole human resource system is constantly improved and adjusted. There must be a strong, aggressive thrust to improve and increase the effectiveness of what is currently being done. Equal attention should also be given to changes that require adjustments in the program. The airplane pilot devotes careful attention to keeping the plane on course in accordance with the prearranged flight plan. But in addition, the pilot knows that if he or she is to arrive at the destination on schedule, he or she must make adjustments when changes occur in the flight characteristics of the plane or in the environment that it is flying through.

Although specific accountability for monitoring and making changes should be assigned to one executive or department, everyone involved must be concerned with making changes. The two most serious errors in effective human resource planning are (1) failure to keep it current, to make adjustments, and to constantly tailor it to meet the changing needs of the enterprise and (2) failure to communicate and achieve support for adjustments made in the plan.

Millions, and perhaps billions, of dollars are wasted annually by corporations that send executives to expensive training programs. They enthusiastically make decisions to engage in really exciting new ventures—professional management, human resource planning, or more effective expense control. Too soon, and too often, the program is initiated with elaborate planning and fanfare only to see interest wane and someone look up a year later and ask, "By the way, what happened to the job performance standards that everyone was supposed to write?" Oh, "Oh, I stopped making the reports regarding personnel changes in my department because they were not made during the three months I was out of the department and no one seemed to know the difference. I just thought that nothing was ever done with them."

There should be no initial commitment to human resource planning unless there is also an equal commitment to continuously improve and update the plan. The plan should never be implemented unless there is both structure and assigned responsibility for its adjustment and change. Management should assume a stewardship responsibility not to waste money or time on projects, including human resource planning, that are later to be aborted or allowed to die of neglect. This can be avoided with appropriate initial planning and continuing attention to the change and administration of the plan.

15

Conclusions

There is a strong conviction that something dynamic and dramatic is happening in the field of human resource accounting and planning. Companies must make revolutionary changes if they expect to take the initiative to ensure human effectiveness today and get ready for tomorrow.

I want to speak on a one-to-one basis with the reader and to clarify the questions remaining—to reemphasize key points in order to ensure conviction and response. As an observer and participant in the complex but inevitable forces at work in our society, I was convinced in 1970 that rights for women would become the most decisive issue in the 1970s and the one requiring the most rethinking and procedural change. It was evident that leadership had stuck its head in the sand during the 1960s when the burning issue was civil rights for blacks, and had suffered serious disruptions as a result. It appeared that the mistake was about to be repeated regarding women, even though the number of women involved, and their financial and political clout, would far overshadow that of the black forces. I wanted to say to corporate management, "Get your house in order. This can be the greatest opportunity ever for employing and promoting well-qualified people. The additional income earned by women will also create vast new markets, thus stimulating growth in the economy and benefiting the company employing women." I also wanted to urge women to be qualified and to merit better jobs, more pay, and greater responsibility. I wrote a book then that was a plea to both women and companies to get ready for what was happening so that there could be mutual achievement of their goals.[1]

[1] Ray A. Killian, *The Working Woman*, AMACOM, 1971.

RESPONDING TO THE HUMAN EMPHASIS

And now, again, the plea has gone forth on another subject. The remaining quarter of this century will be known as the humanistic era. Society and enterprise are shifting their focus from things and quantity to values and the quality of life, the rights of individuals to expect and to receive the "good things of life" from society and companies. The message is intended to emphasize:

—The pervasive cost and influence of the enterprise's human resources.

—That management can and has a right to achieve an ROI from the high and rising cost of human time.

—That effectiveness of current operation and future profitability is dependent on finding better solutions to the total array of human resource challenges.

—That a successful human resource plan must encompass certain key areas: determining needs, ascertaining inventory available, development and training, productivity, leadership, utilization, compensation, and retention.

—That specific, planned strategy should be mapped for successfully initiating, implementing, and administering the human resource plan.

—That appropriate human resource planning can make available to individual employees those conditions and compensations demanded as a condition for their presence and contribution.

—That the benefits of ROI in human resources are financial goal achievement; delivery to customers of consistently high quality products and services; human morality as represented by money, benefits, and psychic income; achievement of corporate short- and long-range continuity and growth goals; and varied contributions to society by a successful company that is able to do so because of its high-quality human resource program.

There has been an attempt to integrate new management strategies for increasing human effectiveness and improving the quality of human life. The emphasis has been to alert management to the great truth that society is change, movement, and new demands. The unprecedented worldwide ferment and storm will not blow over; instead, it will herald the fundamental changes that must occur in our basic human resource system. Causes and forces that are forever gathering strength require alterations not only in society but also in companies. Individuals are increasingly motivated by the conviction that they can alter the nature of their lives and that they have the right to do so. As with the gathering force of most major movements in society, it might be too early at this stage for many to recognize what is happening. But in order to harness and channel the human forces of change, systems must be available that people will find acceptable and beneficial.

READINESS TO CHANGE

Responding to the human requirements of corporate and societal life requires radically new structures and procedures. It means developing new skills for coping with brighter, better-educated associates. It means abandonment of traditional prejudices regarding maverick lifestyles. It means greater tolerance of differing opinions and solutions. During this traditional limbo era, human resource planning becomes even more essential in providing a sense of order and in anticipating future expectations of both company and individual. Properly structured, human resource planning can move forces toward the accommodation of change and the integration of both the work and social environment of the organization.

Although human resource planning, organizing, structuring, and formal programs can make significant contributions to both corporate and individual goals, the tendency to overorganize and overstructure must be avoided. To do so might be even worse than having loose organization. Remember that structure and system must either advance the forces involved toward their goals, or they should be eliminated. Oversystematized formulas often become too burdensome and restrictive. Management must exercise value judgment in determining what is desirable and what is too much.

PUTTING IT ALL TOGETHER

In the kaleidoscope of panaceas passing temptingly before management has been the one of "putting it all together." And in the arena of human resource planning, it is necessary to put it all together before the plan will function.

A large number of pieces of human resource planning have been described in this book. All pieces and steps are essential in "putting it all together." But the whole structure is doomed to failure if management tries to tackle the job by jumping in with both feet to solve isolated human problems. If production is unsatisfactory, the solution too often attempted is putting pressure on employees to produce more. The result is seldom a long-range solution to the problem. But if an effective human resource plan were in operation, it could be instrumental in determining quickly why production is faltering. Possibly, there is too much turnover of experienced employees. Maybe vacations are not staggered properly. Perhaps production employees possess insufficient skills to do the job efficiently. The problem might be one of supervision.

The human resource system should anticipate most problems and prevent them from occurring. For those that do occur, the system should provide quicker, more effective solutions. But before this can happen, the system must be a total composite of all pieces, which have been integrated into a smoothly functioning program. If management expects success from a human resource system, all pertinent influences must be incorporated.

IMPACT ON ACTIVITY AND RESULTS

The operation of a human resource plan should make a difference. It ought to have an impact on all company activity and goal achievement. It should be the catalyst that both initiates activity and produces right results. If it becomes the central core of human action, then it must be the basis for making things happen. It should result in placing a higher priority on people. It should enable management to anticipate human needs more effectively. It should produce a more edifying evaluation and utilization of human resources. Individuals should be achieving profitable productivity quicker. The establishment of test groups can show whether one system of training is superior to another. After supervisors have participated in development programs, results should be compared.

People produce results, and an improved human resource program should improve results. The improved human resource system should move activities forward, closer to goal achievement. Before an ROI in human resources can be realized, there must be favorable impact on the activities and results of the enterprise.

UTILIZING TOP-CALIBER MANAGEMENT SKILLS

The design and implementation of human resource planning is a sophisticated process. It reaches into every facet of the enterprise and involves every individual. It is concerned with production, sales and customer relations. It encompasses long-range planning and effective daily supervision. It establishes the responsibility of the company to the individual and of the individual to the company. It seeks to integrate compensation systems with production goals and human resource supply with corporate demands. It involves setting financial goals and then reaching them through human decisions and activity.

Each of these activities is complex and demanding and requires the integration of human skills, manual systems, EDP, economic variables, short- and long-range considerations, and human uncertainties. All these complex intangibles must be brought together in a single, logical human resource plan, which in turn must be integrated with every other activity in the company. All of these must occur at reasonable cost and be acceptable to all individuals involved.

This might seem like "Mission Impossible," but it is both a possible and a practical solution to the most crucial single problem confronting individual managers and corporate goals. But this does not imply that it is easy or that it can occur without the application of the highest degree of professionalism.

The president of an eight-unit company asked my opinion of professional management. My reply was very favorable, but I added that it was not easy and that it could not be implemented without training, serious effort, and a reasonable amount of time. The president followed my advice and attended a professional management briefing. He then sent the company's five vice-presidents to the same briefing. The president became so enchanted with the possibilities of professional management that he requested creeds be written, organizational charts drawn, position descriptions written, standards of performance prepared, and other part of the program completed within 60 days. One of the vice-presidents telephoned me in a panic. My advice was to go slow and never to abandon what had been successful until a better method had proved itself. Impatience for immediate implementation will often result in serious errors and disruption of the ongoing operation of the business.

The same advice applies to the use of professional management in the design and implementation of the human resource plan. True, professional management is necessary, but also required are patience, time, training, testing, revising, and communicating. This doesn't mean undue delays, but it does accept the fact that it is better to take additional time and exert painstaking effort all along the way to ensure that the final plan will be effective in achieving predicted results.

CHECKLIST FOR MAXIMIZING ROI

The following checkpoints are provided to help the manager evaluate the status of human resource planning in the organization. The objective is to identify any areas that could be improved by additional planning.

1. The actual status of human resource planning throughout the organization. Check activity related to human resource planning. Certain human relations progress should be occurring on a continuous basis, or it can be assumed that the plan is in trouble.

2. The adequacy of the information system regarding the availability of human resources.

3. The anticipation of needs far enough in advance to allow for internal succession or outside recruitment.

4. The establishment of meaningful, but ambitious, objectives for the human resource program.

5. The measurement of productivity and effectiveness of managers and workers.

6. The integration of the human resource program into the overall objectives of the organization.

7. The investigation and correction of serious human resource problems.

8. The anticipation of organizational changes and preparation for consequences affecting human resources.

9. The provision for meaningful job placement and promotional procedures.

10. Adequate appraisal of the qualifications and potential of all employees for pay and promotional purposes.

11. Effective control of absenteeism and turnover.

12. Development of qualified replacements for most positions.

13. Identification and communication of job-mobility patterns —promotions and transfers.

14. Motivation of managers and employees to engage in committed job effort.

15. Recruitment of entry-level employees (junior executive trainees and workers) who can be developed and promoted.

16. An acceptable level of recruitment from the outside, for positions higher than entry types, so that employee morale will not be lowered.

17. Attention to career charting and individual development in order to prevent obsolescence and to keep individuals moving forward and upward.

18. Evidence that the human planning system is receiving the support and participation of leadership throughout the company.

19. Timetables for testing whether activities are occurring and results being achieved.

20. Follow-up to ensure that all plan changes and corrective action called for are being taken.

Human resource planning leaders will be able to add to this list, but it is a beginning. Users of the human resource plan should be consulted constantly. What do they like and what don't they like? How should it be changed? When they have been consulted and have participated in the design and implementation of the plan, they will be more likely to accept and support it.

OPERATING IN A HUMAN RESOURCE ENVIRONMENT

The most chilling (or possibly comforting) thought to managers is that the ultimate destiny of the enterprise rests in the hands of individual employees. The production employee has the freedom to determine the quality, and often the quantity, of what he or she does. The salesperson controls whether the sale is made. The department manager determines the effectiveness of the department operation.

Regardless of our advanced degree of automation and use of computers, it is still human choice by individuals that causes activity and results to occur. People are not robots locked into a system over which they have no influence. Rather, they are enlightened; they have individual expectations; they bring to the job unique attitudes and talents; and they want the type of personal affirmation that most job relations are capable of providing.

Operating effectively in the human era means changing the way the company and its people are managed. It means a world within the company that is caught in the crosscurrents of demands —company, employee, legal, and societal. Companies and their leaders have the difficult task of deciding when and how much response should be given. The ebb flow varies, with different emphasis almost daily. It forces companies to examine their basic structure, their philosophies, their supervisory training programs, their grievance procedures, their system of evaluating employees, their staffing methods, and the whole human resources "ball of wax."

The Industrial Revolution, the development of the assembly line, the arrival of automation, and the utilization of the computer caused such drastic changes in the business and industrial world that it will never be the same again. The human era, resulting from the human revolution, is causing even deeper, more drastic changes. Companies are now finding it difficult to justify hiring and promoting those people who, in their opinion, are best qualified. They must use new criteria for determining what the job is worth in relation to other jobs. They find it difficult to discharge employees for what have previously been justifiable reasons. They are attempting to employ and move into various employee classifications throughout the company a certain percentage of women and blacks. They are, in many instances, getting equal or better-qualified employees in connection with affirmative action programs; but this might also mean employing less-qualified personnel, providing more training, and settling for less production. So the human era might also mean that the company is not able to do what it considers best for the business.

COPING WITH CHANGES

Our fluid, free, and open society has led people to believe that they are entitled to the good life and that they should be able to exercise control over that life, including what happens on the job. Their loyalties, interests, and priorities have shifted from the company they work for to the outside world. They are less concerned with traditions and what happened in the past than people used to be, and so, as employees, they care little about how the company got started and what was successful for the founder.

The composition of the workforce has changed from largely all-white males to a balanced mixture that includes women, blacks, and older workers. The government has increased its control over company policies and practices relating to people—employees have more "entitlements" and are guaranteed greater benefits, so increasingly company employees look to the government to make certain they get from the job what they are entitled to.

We must find ways to work more effectively in the context of the new work ethic and today's criteria for success by enabling employees to participate meaningfully in decision making and company concerns that might affect their lives. We must test all decisions and proposed actions for their probable impacts on people. Many companies have learned to their regret that what is economically feasible and traditionally reasonable suddenly turns sour when employees and community groups oppose it. Finally, we must accept that today's best leadership qualities involve high risk to the economic, legal, and employee relations of the company.

Companies must cope *now* with these issues. They are not threats or possibilities of what might happen at some foggy point in future years. The effectiveness and survival of the company today will be substantially affected by the way management handles them.

PLANNING TO MEET TOMORROW'S DEMANDS

Get ready for tomorrow before it runs over you! Looking back to the "good old days" is time wasted. Things will never be the same, regardless of fluctuating economic conditions. Even good answers today will not last forever. The most dramatic and drastic changes regarding tomorrow's company world will occur in matters relating to human resources. New, more innovative and effective ways must be devised for linking company interest with employee self-interest. The company can make quicker and more controlled changes regarding products and finances than it can regarding people. To a considerable extent, company policies, procedures, compensation rates, benefits, and treatment of people must be similar to those in other companies. Competition for employees makes this advisable, and numerous government regulations require it.

What, then, are the options available to the company? How should it plan to meet tomorrow's demands? The only reasonable solution means anticipating realistically what tomorrow's human resource environment will be. A comprehensive, detailed, flexible, and realistic human resource plan should be developed to meet those demands. This should include appropriate consideration for coping with:

—Designing and finding better solutions to the rigidities of organization structure and authority.

—Ways to merit individual presence on the job and full commitment to job goals.

—More effective feedback and quicker response to employee needs.

—More effective utilization of employees' minds, talents, and potential.

—Changing leadership styles and techniques to more effectively deal with increased education and expectations.

—Counteracting employee uneasiness, suspicion, frustration, and lack of confidence in the company and its management.

—Finding viable substitutes for the loss of authority and traditional forms of motivation.

Although some of these items might seem like dire predictions, that is not the case. In reality, most of these represent vast new opportunities for companies, as well as benefits for employees. Leaders will have available greatly enlarged education, talent, and potential assets to draw upon. The human environment on the job will never be the same for supervisors, employees, or company. But it can be much better. Working with brighter, more innovative people can be exciting. Finding new forms of organization and solutions to work ethics can be challenging and satisfying. Tomorrow's human resource work environment has the potential for more stimulating rewards for everyone concerned. But for this to happen, the highest quality of human resource planning must constantly anticipate changes and cope effectively with them as they occur. A vital part of this plan must be preparing people to meet the needs and conditions of the future. Collectively, enterprises—ranging from farms to factories—and their people can have a significant impact on what the future will be. Concentration on inventing futures, rather than reflecting on past memories, can provide the planning framework for future modeling and simulation. It is important that enterprises and their human and material resources be aggressively channeled toward making the job and the environment favorable to people. The interest of both company and individual will be subjected to hazardous uncertainty when constructive leadership is lacking. But total concern should involve and marshal the commitment of every employee. The company's and the individual's entitlement to "doing their thing" should motivate the development of a world in which it can occur.

THE FUTURE OF HUMAN RESOURCE PLANNING

Effective human resource planning today means people and company power tomorrow. The future of the enterprise and the future of human resource planning will likely go down the same path. No company will be successful unless it finds solutions to its people problems, and those solutions will be available only through a comprehensive, well-designed human resource plan.

To anticipate changes and get the best solutions, an organized systematic approach must be taken. The future of human resource planning will involve:

1. Assigning human resource planning to a top-level executive reporting directly to the chief executive of the corporation.

2. Giving as much attention to human resource planning as is traditionally given to production, marketing, and financial planning.

3. Integrating human resource planning into every facet of the enterprise.

4. Testing all major corporate decisions and contemplated action for its human impact—both inside and outside the company.

5. Allocating time, funds, and priorities to human resource planning in accordance with its decisive importance on the continuity and profitability of the enterprise.

6. Making full use of EDP and all other systems and resources for the benefit of human resource planning.

7. Exerting maximum effort to communicate the intent, the procedures, and the achievements of human resource planning as a benefit for managers and employees.

8. Exercising increased company discipline to ensure that the plan is viable and that it is being fully supported by everyone who exercises authority.

9. Fully utilizing the latest findings and techniques of behavioral science, management theory, professional management, and technology in improving the quality of human resource planning.

10. Engaging in constant research, comparison, improvement, and testing of results to ensure that the plan is achieving the goals set for it.

This is a big challenge, but appropriate human resource planning is equal to it. People and corporations working together can accomplish what they commit themselves to do. Each new day provides exciting opportunities to grow, to plan better, and to bring about enriched affirmation in self and others.

Certain government enforcement agencies repeatedly emphasize that their test in determining whether a company is in compliance with the law is "not intent, but results." It is also an appropriate test of the ROI human resource planning concept. It must make an identifiable contribution to the financial goals of the enterprise. It must result in better treatment of people and improved employee relations. It must produce a better return on the investment in human time. And it must improve productivity.

Management dares ignore the benefits of ROI in human resource planning only at its own peril.